Quick Diamond Quilts
& beyond

12 SPARKLING PROJECTS • BEGINNER-FRIENDLY TECHNIQUES

JAN KRENTZ

C&T PUBLISHING

Text copyright © 2010 by Jan Krentz

Artwork copyright © 2010 by C&T Publishing, Inc.

Publisher: Amy Marson

Creative Director: Gailen Runge

Acquisitions Editor: Susanne Woods

Editor: Karla Menaugh

Technical Editors: Ellen Pahl and Sandy Peterson

Copyeditor/Proofreader: Wordfirm Inc.

Cover Designer: Kristen Yenche

Page Layout Artist: Kristen Yenche

Book Designer: Rose Sheifer-Wright

Production Coordinator: Zinnia Heinzmann

Production Editor: Julia Cianci

Illustrator: Tim Manibusan

Photography by Christina Carty-Francis and Diane Pedersen of C&T Publishing, Inc., unless otherwise noted.

Published by C&T Publishing, Inc., P.O. Box 1456, Lafayette, CA 94549

Library of Congress Cataloging-in-Publication Data

Krentz, Jan P., 1955-

Quick diamond quilts & beyond : 12 sparkling projects, beginner-friendly techniques / by Jan Krentz.

  p. cm.

Includes bibliographical references.

ISBN 978-1-57120-581-0 (soft cover)

1. Patchwork--Patterns. 2. Quilting. I. Title.

TT835.K7684 2010

746.46'041--dc22

                    2009020113

Printed in China

10 9 8 7 6 5 4 3 2 1

acknowledgments:

I want to thank each quilter and editor who made this collection of quilt designs as exciting and inspiring as it is! A book is as rich as the contributors whose work appears within.

Special recognition goes to each quiltmaker and machine quilter: Betty Alofs, Anna Mae Bach, Kathy Butler, B.J. Coopes, Mary Beth Craig, Frances Cunningham, Jan Darnell, Carol Gilbert, Jacqueline Lacey, Lynne Lichtenstern, Sue Mezera, D'Andrea Mitchell, Lee Olson, Carolyn Reynolds, Nancy Rowland, Jane Sassaman, Cindy Stearns, Janet Sturdevant Stuart, Suzanne Taylor, Patricia Votruba, Amy Wazny, Pat Wolfe, and Julia Zgliniec.

Thank you to the C&T editors, graphics designers, and photographers whose expertise made this book shine! I am blessed to have had Karla Menaugh, Ellen Pahl, and Sandy Peterson edit the text and verify the pattern calculations. Thanks to Kristen Yenche, Zinnia Heinzmann, Julia Cianci, Tim Manibusan, Christina Carty-Francis, and Diane Pedersen for your workmanship, inspiration, and artistry.

dedication:

With thanks to my loving husband Don and our family: Ryan, Tanya, Dan, Lindsay, and Ryan O.

contents

introduction

I enjoy making and using quilts! Traditional pieced designs are especially appealing to me, and pieced patterns are a great way to learn the skills required to make larger or more complex designs.

For years I have explored eight-pointed star designs and related patterns. While creating one quilt, I am often struck with inspiration for numerous additional quilts—resulting in a series of eight-pointed star designs and diamond quilts. The patterns in this book are based upon traditional designs made in a larger scale. My previous book, *Quick Star Quilts and Beyond*, featured 20 patterns for colorful, fun star quilts on a grand scale. This book features more 45° diamond patterns that are guaranteed to get you sewing and reduce your fabric stash!

Creating detailed geometric patterns can be challenging. Artists who are new to quiltmaking will enjoy this lighthearted pattern collection featuring larger shapes, with some easy piecing options, and fresh fabric combinations. Seasoned quilt-makers will enjoy the attractive designs that piece together in a relatively short time.

The designs in this collection begin with the 45° diamond, or parallelogram. This shape has two opposing parallel edges, and all four sides are of equal length. It differs from its "half-square" or right-angle counterpart, whose four sides are not equal. The designs created from the true diamond are more appealing to me.

You can use 45° diamonds in a variety of patterns, including one-patch designs. Smaller and larger diamonds may be combined in the same composition for variety and interest. The diamonds can also be altered in appearance when pieced, or when cut specially to feature prominent fabric motifs.

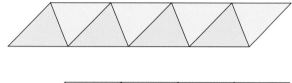

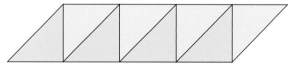

A row of split diamonds made from true 45° diamonds (top) and a similar row of split diamonds made with half-square right triangles (bottom)

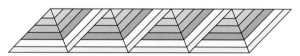

A row of striped diamonds: mirror-image halves cut with the half-diamond ruler

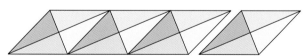

Quarter-diamond units create dimensional effects when cut from light and dark values.

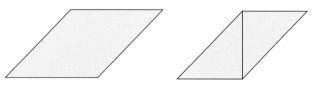

A 45° diamond or parallelogram (left) compared with a half-square diamond unit (right)

Versatile 45° diamonds are used in a variety of patterns. If you cut the diamond shapes in half or in quarters with additional seams, you create a myriad of new design possibilities. Other piecing options provide unlimited variations.

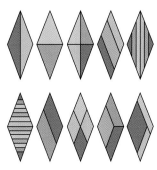

Pieced 45° diamonds

Another way to dramatically alter the appearance of the basic shape is to carefully cut the full or partial diamonds to feature prominent stripes or fabric motifs. This is known as *fussy cutting*.

When creating my own quilt designs, I find it easier to cut perfect diamonds with acrylic rulers designed for that purpose. Two different sets of diamond rotary cutting tools are available from C&T Publishing for easy measurement and cutting. (See Resources, page 95.)

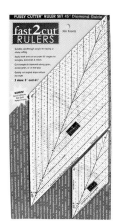

The project instructions in this book include materials lists and assembly directions for making easy quilts with the fast2cut Fussy Cutter 45° diamond, fast2cut half-diamond and quarter-diamond rulers or with traditional templates that you can make yourself from the template patterns provided on the pullout pages.

I know you will enjoy the wide range of attractive quick diamond quilt patterns and will be inspired by the exciting designs of the quilt artists in the Diamond Gallery, pages 38–53. Have fun making the quilts and sharing your talents and creativity with those you love!

Happy stitching!

Jan P. Krentz

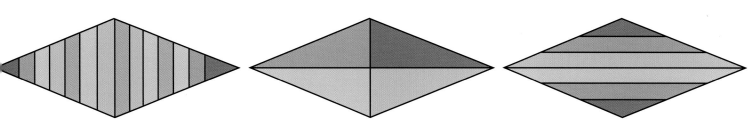

fabric selection

A fabric collection with calm, solid, and low-contrast designs;
add an unexpected contrasting color for interest

Your fabric selection has a great influence on the project's appearance. This obvious statement has deeper meaning!

The quilt projects in this book feature large shapes and pieces, requiring minimal cutting and piecing. Selecting quiet, calm, solid, or tone-on-tone fabrics will result in a very large graphic design with low visual interest—in other words: a boring quilt. The surface will have little of the visual energy that a patterned fabric would provide.

Enhance the quilt design with changes in value (lightness to darkness), texture, and contrast. Adding small bits of unexpected colors will provide excitement and interest to a calm fabric collection.

Focus Fabrics

Fabrics with medium- and large-scale pattern designs provide the themes for the projects in this book. These are the "stars" of the projects; the larger the print or pattern scale, the more dramatic the design will be! Select one large-scale print as the theme or focus fabric. Determine the placement for this fabric in your project. You may need to fussy cut or select certain motifs from the print. Position the ruler over that motif and cut out single elements for the project.

jan's tip

Be sure to purchase adequate yardage when selecting a fabric with a large-scale design. Quilt borders and fussy-cut, identical motifs require more yardage than allover patterns. I typically purchase four to six yards of any large-scale print when I have no specific project in mind. I purchase more yardage if the fabric is suitable for a large project. Remember: fabric designs are printed in limited quantity, they sell out rapidly, and they are rarely reprinted.

Examples of large-scale focus fabrics

Fussy cutting specific motifs (printed elements)
from a focus fabric.
Flip templates over to cut mirror image pieces.

Select additional fabrics that coordinate
with the large-scale focus fabric—fabrics
with smaller print scales, different patterns or textures, and varying colors.
Include a surprise color in a small quantity for interest and excitement. Use
these bright surprise colors, sometimes
called *zingers*, in limited quantities. If
the project fabrics do not include any
zingers, you can add narrow trim in
a contrasting color or pattern to add
interest or define a design area.

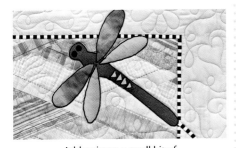

Add a *zinger*: a small bit of
unexpected color or pattern.

Detail: narrow contrasting strip
inserted at the seamline

Interesting Calm Fabrics

This category of fabrics supports the focus fabric. When viewed from a distance, the
subtle pattern or lower contrast within the fabric complements the focus fabric. Calm
fabrics, such as tone-on-tone blenders and monochromatic prints (prints with several
shades and tints of just one color), provide a resting place for the eye and frequently
create a cohesive background behind the focus fabric.

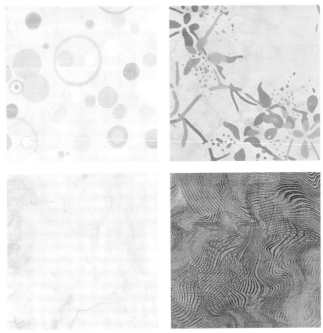

Interesting calm fabric prints and batik patterns

Stripes and Geometrics

These two fabric styles provide line and texture within
the design and can be used effectively to add design
interest. The patterns may be printed, dyed, or constructed
by sewing several strips together to create a strip set.

Using an interesting large-scale stripe within large shapes
is very exciting! The fabric can be cut so that the stripe
parallels an outer edge, creating a border, or so that the
stripe bisects the shape in various ways.

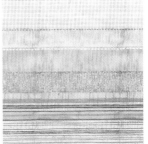
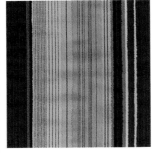

Large-scale printed and dyed stripes

Smaller-scale or subtle or low-contrast stripes and gradations can also serve as calm fabrics, creating a contrast to a large-scale focus fabric, or they can be used as narrow trim strips to enhance and visually separate two design areas.

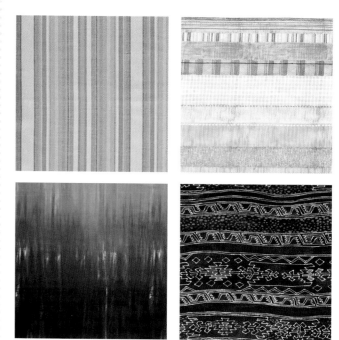

Subtle or low-contrast printed and woven stripes and gradations

Examples of subtle stripes in various quilts

Striped fabrics incorporated within half diamonds or
Faux Diamond rectangles

Geometric designs include any patterns that are regular repeats of lines, squares, triangles, stars, circles, dots, checks, and so on. The designs provide visual activity or filling for the quilt, and are companions to the focus fabric and the interesting calm fabrics.

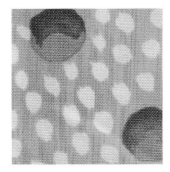
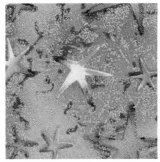

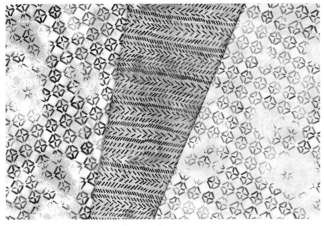

Geometric patterns

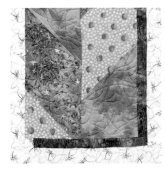

Examples of geometric patterns within the pieced designs

Prewashing Guidelines

Today's cotton fabrics, purchased from a reputable quilt shop, are high-quality, medium-weight cotton, with a good tight weave. I frequently sew my projects using unwashed yardage, with excellent results. Fabrics purchased from discount stores or large chain stores may vary in quality.

In the past, fabrics often had a tendency to shrink significantly and lose excess dye when washed the first time. It was therefore a common practice to prewash all fabrics prior to using them. It is still advisable to prewash the following fabric types:

- Hand-woven fabrics such as madras plaid, Guatemalan stripes, or other ethnic fabric that you know to be hand-woven or hand-printed

- Loosely woven fabrics such as homespun, some flannels, plaids, and brocade

- Hand-dyed fabrics or batiks, especially supersaturated colors (anything medium to dark in value)

- Any blend or specialty fabric that you are unfamiliar with (If you do not know how it will appear or behave after laundering, wash it to find out before using it in your quilt.)

Laundering will remove the factory finishes applied to the fabric. When washing fabrics that have been dyed (such as hand-dyed, batik, tie-dyed, or shibori), add a color stabilizer such as Synthrapol, Retayne, or Dharma Dye Fixative. Another option is to add a product designed to absorb excess dye molecules in the water, such as Shout Color Catcher, Woolite Dye Magnet, or Zero Dye Magnet (Canada). For more information, see Resources, page 95.

Typically, the fabric will require light pressing after laundering to smooth out the wrinkles. An optional light mist of starch or fabric finish will add body to limp fabrics. If you use starch, add it just before working with the fabrics, and wash the project immediately after construction to avoid attracting insects that are drawn to starch. I do not recommend storing yardage that contains starch.

jan's tip
Evaluate your fabrics, and if you are in doubt, I suggest prewashing them before cutting them for your project.

tools and equipment

Sewing Equipment

Sewing Machine

- Straight stitch (suitable for seams in patchwork)
- Multiple stitches (if you are planning to do machine appliqué)

Sewing Machine Accessories

- Single-hole throat plate (provides a better stitch quality, particularly when sewing seams at the narrow tips of diamonds)
- Zigzag throat plate (for decorative stitching)
- Quarter-inch foot (to achieve an accurate seam width)
- Open-toe appliqué foot (for any pattern with appliqué)
- Walking foot (may be necessary for piecing on bias edges)

Cutting Equipment

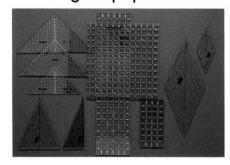

- Large or oversized cutting mat
- fast2cut Fussy Cutter 45° 6½" and 3" diamond rulers
- fast2cut Fussy Cutter 45° 6½" diamond, half-diamond, and quarter rulers

- Rotary cutter with sharp blade
- Several acrylic rulers designed for rotary cutting (I advise using products by the same manufacturer if possible.)

  6½" × 24" ruler or 6" × 24" ruler
  6" × 12" ruler
  4" × 8" ruler
  Triangle ruler (90°-45°-45°)
  Quilter's square ruler (12" × 12" or larger)

- Templates from stiff template plastic (optional)
- Omnigrid Invisi-Grip (optional)
- Sandpaper dots (optional)

Diamond Rulers

fast2cut Fussy Cutter 45° diamond rulers: 6½" and 3"

fast2cut Half- and Quarter-Diamond Ruler Set

Sewing Notions

- Thread snips
- Seam ripper
- Sewing awl or stilleto
- Extra fine (silk-weight) glass-head pins for precision piecing
- Sharp (not universal or ballpoint) sewing machine needles, size 10 or 12 (70 or 80), designed for sewing seams in woven fabrics
- Medium- to heavyweight template plastic (optional)
- Pencil and permanent marking pen
- Isopropyl alcohol pads, in foil packaging, to remove ink from rulers

Pressing Equipment

- Iron
- Ironing board
- Spray starch or fabric finish
- Pump spray water bottle
- Distilled water (optional)

Use a steam iron that functions with or without water, allowing different types of pressing. Always press the fabric in an up-and-down motion to prevent stretching or distorting.

Geometric Components: 45° Diamonds, Quarter and Half Diamonds

The patterns in this book use two different sets of rulers designed specifically for cutting diamonds. (See Diamond Rulers, page 10) The rulers are designed for easy measurement and rotary cutting. If you prefer, you can create plastic templates for tracing the shapes onto the fabric to cut with scissors. (Template patterns are on the pullout pages.) A big advantage of the diamond rulers is the ability to safely rotary cut against them.

The two sizes of diamonds most commonly used throughout this book are referred to by their unfinished size: most are 6½" and 3". That is the distance from one parallel side to the other. The finished sizes of the diamonds are 6" and 2½". If you want to cut diamonds from strips, you would cut 6½" strips for the larger diamonds and 3" strips for the smaller diamonds. My book *Quick Star Quilts and Beyond* features eight-pointed star designs with radial centers; they use the same size diamonds and half diamonds.

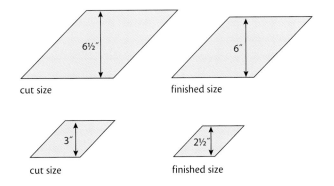

cut size   6½"

finished size   6"

cut size   3"

finished size   2½"

Cutting with Scissors

1. Trace around the diamond or partial diamond template or ruler with a pencil or extra-fine permanent pen.

2. Cut along the lines with sewing scissors. Cut directly on the drawn line or just *inside* the line to avoid making the shapes larger than they should be.

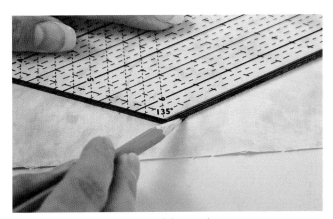

Trace around the template.

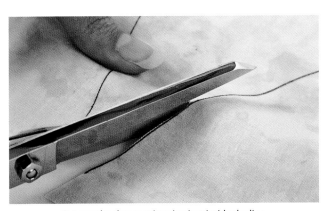

Cut out the shapes, trimming just inside the line.

Rotary Cutting

When you are rotary cutting, I recommend that you use one of the products below to help your ruler grip the fabric and prevent slipping.

- *Invisi-Grip*. Cut the film slightly smaller than your ruler size. Place it on the underside of the ruler.

- *Adhesive-backed sandpaper dots*. Cut each dot in half. Adhere the half dots to the ruler bottom on each tip and edge to add stability.

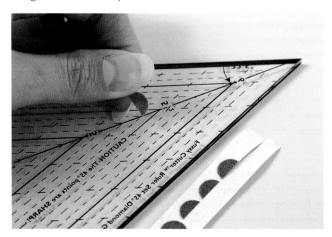

- *Steam-A-Seam 2* or *Steam-A-Seam Lite*. Cut a narrow strip or two, and remove the paper backing. Center the strip on the ruler bottom, and adhere it by simply pressing it with your hand; the pebbly, slightly sticky surface will provide stability.

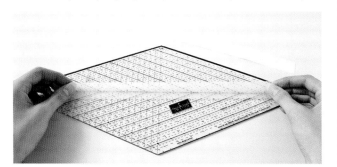

STRIP METHOD

This is the simplest method. Use it when you want several diamonds cut from the same fabric without regard to motifs or designs. Diamonds cut this way will have two straight-grain edges and two bias edges. The available width of fabric strips is assumed to be approximately 42" from selvage to selvage.

1. Cut 6½" strips for the larger diamond and 3" strips for the smaller diamond.

2. Open the strips so they are not folded; layer 2 or 3 strips right side up when striped diamonds need to be angeled the same direction for the project. Layer the opened strips wrong sides together to cut pairs of diamonds with mirrored angled strip effect. Align the sides of the diamond ruler with the edges of the strip, and cut along the diagonal ends. Continue cutting across the strip until you have the number of diamonds you need.

- 1 fabric strip 6½" × 42" (cut selvage to selvage) will yield 3 diamonds.

- 1 fabric strip 3" × 42" (cut selvage to selvage) will yield 8 or 9 diamonds.

CUT-AND-ROTATE METHOD

1. Place a full or partial diamond ruler on the fabric. The fabric may be single or multiple layers, but I suggest no more than 4 layers for accurate cutting. Cut around the edge(s) on the far side of the ruler away from your body with a rotary cutter.

2. Rotate the shape on the cutting mat to comfortably cut the remaining edges, or rotate the mat. A turntable-style cutting mat is useful for cutting smaller diamonds or partial diamonds.

BUDDY RULER TECHNIQUE

1. Position the diamond ruler (or partial diamond ruler) on the fabric. Cut around the edge(s) on the far side of the ruler away from your body with a rotary cutter as shown in Step 1, for the cut-and-rotate method.

2. Align a second "buddy ruler" along the forward edge of the shape being cut. Hold it securely in place, and carefully slide the diamond ruler aside slightly. Cut against the buddy ruler. Realign the diamond ruler with the cut edges, and repeat the process with the buddy ruler to cut the remaining edge. Do not inadvertently cut into the diamond shape.

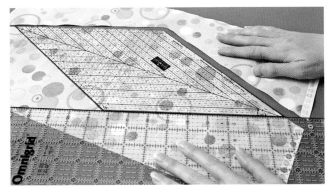

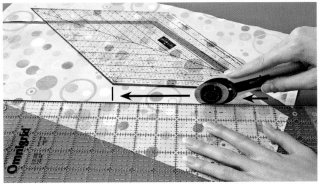

FUSSY CUTTING MOTIFS

1. Position the large diamond ruler over a motif in the fabric.

2. Trace the key design elements onto the ruler with a permanent pen, such as a Sharpie or Identi-pen. The marks can be easily removed later with rubbing alcohol or a plastic eraser.

3. After you have cut the first diamond, use the markings on the ruler to help you correctly position the ruler on the printed fabric so you can fussy cut additional diamonds.

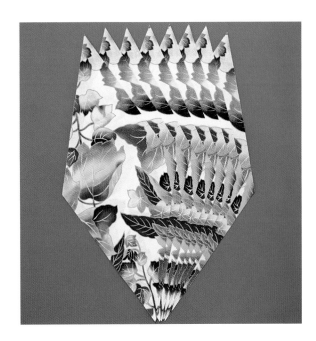

CUTTING DIAMONDS FROM STRIPES

Cutting with the Template

1. Working with striped fabric or a pieced strip set, layer the fabric wrong sides together with the stripes aligned.

2. Align a long straight ruler (6½″ × 24″ or 6″ × 24″) with a stripe or seamline. Cut strips 3″ or 6½″ wide—the same width as the diamond template you plan to use.

3. Align the diamond template with the cut edges of the fabric strip. Cut diamonds from the fabric strips. Layer fabric strips wrong sides together to cut mirror image diamonds.

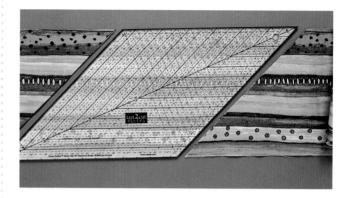

Cutting with a Straight Ruler

1. Follow Steps 1 and 2 above. Then rotate the long straight ruler, aligning the 45° guide at the cut edge of the strip.

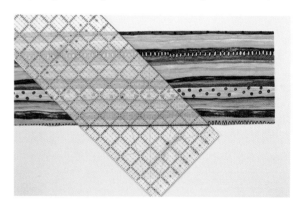

2. Cut the diamonds the *same width* as the strips. Watch the grainline of the diamond shape. Two edges should be parallel with the stripe, on the straight grain; 2 edges should be true 45° bias. Layer fabric strips wrong sides together to cut mirror-image diamonds.

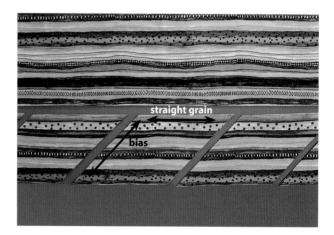

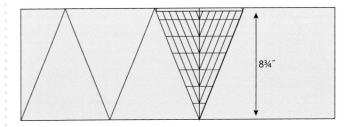

CUTTING HALF DIAMONDS

Option 1: Cut Full Diamonds in Half

Cut full diamond shapes, and then subcut the diamonds in half horizontally through all the layers, creating half diamonds. Note: When you sew 2 of these half diamonds together, they will be smaller than those cut using the original 6½" or 3" diamond, due to the center seam allowance.

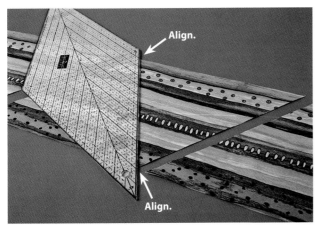

Cut corner to corner.

Option 2: Use the Half-Diamond Ruler

You can place the half-diamond ruler horizontally, vertically, or with one side aligned with a pattern in the fabric, depending on the effect you wish to achieve.

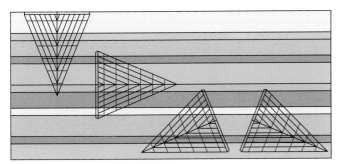

You can vary the placement of the half-diamond ruler to accentuate your fabric.

To cut 6½" half diamonds without regard to a fabric print or stripe, cut a strip 8¾" wide. Place the 6½" half-diamond ruler with the short side along one long cut edge of the fabric, cut out, and then rotate the ruler for alternating cuts. This will give you straight grain along the short side. You can also cut 6½" strips and place the long side of the ruler along the cut edge of the fabric; the straight grain will be parallel to one long side. Consider the fabric print or motif, the quilt design, and the number of half diamonds you need to determine which strip width to cut.

8¾"

Cutting Half Diamonds for Mirror-Image Designs

1. Layer fabric strips with wrong sides together, matching the stripes, to cut mirror-image pieces. For 6½" half diamonds, cut strips 6½" wide. Align the longer edge of the half-diamond ruler with the strip edge. Cut half diamonds, rotating the ruler for alternating cuts.

2. Position the 2 diamond halves right sides up with the shortest edges touching. The complete diamond shape should form a mirror-image pattern; if you're using a stripe, it will create a V or chevron pattern.

3. Join the half diamonds together in pairs, creating pieced 45° diamonds. Press the center seams open to eliminate bulk.

Half-diamond shapes cut from layered fabrics have mirror-image patterns.

Jan's tip

A benefit of using a half-diamond ruler is that a seam allowance has been added to the ruler. When you sew together two half-diamonds cut from a fast2cut half-diamond ruler, you will produce a full-size diamond that will match whole diamonds cut from the 3" or 6½" diamond rulers.

Cutting Half Diamonds of Special Sizes

When making my *Indian Summer* Thousand Pyramids quilt (page 92), or when working with other traditional patterns such as a Kaleidoscope, Rocky Road to Kansas, Moorish Cross, Signal, or Harbor Lights, you might need to cut an odd-sized half diamond. To cut these shapes with the half-diamond ruler, follow these steps.

1. Draw 1 block, full size.

2. Place the half-diamond ruler upside down on top of the half-diamond pattern, aligning the ¼" dashed line of the ruler with the pointy 45° tip and the sides of the pattern. Draw around the ruler to add the ¼" seam allowance on all 3 sides with a fine, sharp pencil.

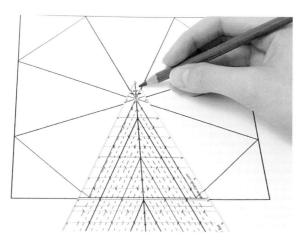

3. Mark the printed side of the half-diamond ruler according to the penciled seam allowance from the pattern. Use a permanent marker or an adhesive guide such as a strip of blue painter's tape, moleskin, fluorescent tape, or vinyl cling strips to make the base line of the triangle.

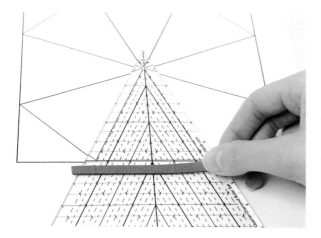

4. Align the guide with a cleanly cut straight edge of the fabric, and cut along the remaining 2 edges.

jan's tip

You can use my Quilter's Design Mirrors to preview framed diamond designs. Place the longest edge of the quarter diamond ruler on a stripe, then place the hinge of the design mirror at the 90-degree corner, with the 2 mirror tiles aligned with the 2 shorter sides of the quarter diamond ruler. You'll see the framed diamond design and can audition the best spot to cut your quarter diamond. The photograph shows how the mirrors give you a complete view of a Lone Star block when you have just two of the diamonds completed. It works the same way for any stripe or print fabric, allowing you to audition your fabric before cutting.

Making a Tape Guide

Create guides from painter's adhesive tape. They are inexpensive, easy to make, and won't leave adhesive residue on your tools.

TOOLS

3M or Scotch brand blue painter's tape from a hardware or office supply store, a cutting mat, an acrylic ruler, and a utility knife with a new blade. For safety: DO NOT USE A ROTARY CUTTER!!!

1. *Hold the roll of tape in your hand.*

2. *Cut into the tape with a utility knife, stroking with firm pressure across the width of the tape. Make several strokes, cutting slightly deeper into the tape with each stroke.*

3. *Move the blade about 2" away from the first cut. Repeat the process.*

4. *Peel off a thick stack of tape. Place the sticky side down on your cutting mat. Cut into narrower widths— ¼", ⅜", or ½" as preferred. Use the tape guides on the bottoms of your rulers or in front of your presser foot to act as a guide when cutting or sewing.*

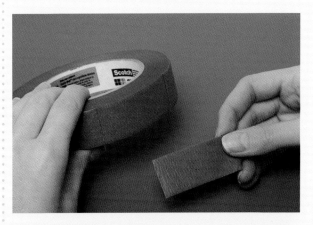

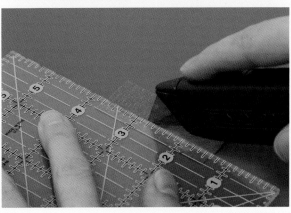

CREATING EASY SPLIT DIAMONDS

Diamonds Split Lengthwise

Diamonds cut in half lengthwise are known as long half diamonds.

1. Cut 2 different fabric strips 4½" wide from selvage to selvage for the 6½" diamond; cut 2 strips 2¾" wide from selvage to selvage for the 3" diamond.

2. Place the strips right sides together. Sew together along 1 long edge. Press the seam open.

3. Lay the diamond ruler on the strip set, aligning the lengthwise centerline of the ruler with the seam. Cut diamonds 1 at a time from the pieced strips; do not overcut into the surrounding fabric.

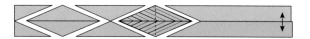

4. Remove the stitching from the remainder of the seam (of the strip set).

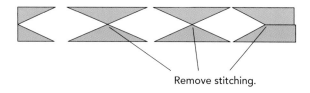

Remove stitching.

5. Place the fabric right sides together once again. Sew the remaining long edges together. Press the seam open. Cut additional diamonds from this combination.

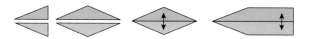

- 2 strips 4½" × 42" sewn together typically yield 3 to 4 split 6½" diamonds.

- 2 strips 2½" × 42" sewn together typically yield 8 split 3" diamonds.

Diamonds Split Crosswise

1. Cut 2 different fabric strips 9½" wide from selvage to selvage for the 6½" diamond; cut 2 strips 5" wide from selvage to selvage for the 3" diamond.

2. Place the strips right sides together. Sew together along 1 long edge. Press the seam open.

3. Lay the diamond ruler on the fabric, aligning the crosswise centerline of the ruler with the seam. Cut diamonds 1 at a time from the pieced strips; do not overcut into the surrounding fabric.

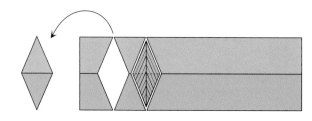

4. Remove the stitching from the remainder of the seam. (See Step 4, Diamonds Split Lengthwise, above.)

5. Place the fabric right sides together once again. Sew the remaining long edge together. Press the seam open. Cut diamonds from this combination.

- 2 strips 9½" × 42" (cut selvage to selvage) typically yield 9–10 split 6½" diamonds.

- 2 strips 2½" × 42" (cut selvage to selvage) typically yield 23–24 split 3" diamonds.

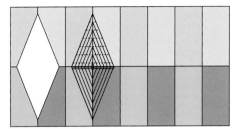

Diamonds Split into Quarters

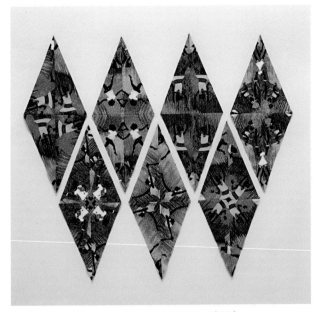

Fussy-cut diamonds are created with
4 quarter-diamond sections.

There are several ways to cut using the quarter-diamond ruler to create different effects.

- To feature a design in the fabric, trace fabric motifs by drawing an outline on the ruler's surface with a permanent marker such as a Sharpie or Identi-pen. Align the ruler with the traced outline on the yardage. Cut several of the same image, 1 at a time. (See Fussy Cutting Motifs, page 13)

- To fussy cut mirror-image pieces, flip the ruler wrong side up. Align the outline over the fabric motif, and cut the reverse quarter-diamond shape.

- For simple mirror images, layer the fabric wrong sides together before cutting with the quarter-diamond ruler.

- For easy sewing (to avoid piecing quarter diamonds together), first sew oversized rectangles together. Press the seams open or to the side. Then position the diamond ruler over the intersection of 4 rectangles, and cut around all 4 sides.

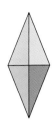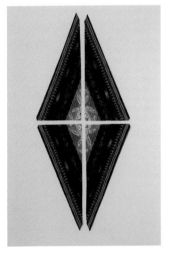

- For a repeating outline or framed effect, cut striped fabrics with the quarter-diamond ruler, aligning the longest edge with the stripe. When 4 quarter diamonds are combined, the finished diamond will appear to have a repeating outline or frame. These remind me of the yarn-and-stick crafts I made as a Girl Scout, known as "God's Eyes" or "Ojos de Dios."

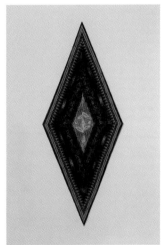

Cutting Angled Strips for Framed Diamonds

This cutting technique can be used to cut a large quantity of angled shapes, which is helpful when you are making large quilts.

Tools

- 2 rulers 6½" × 24" or 2 rulers 6" × 24"
- 6½" diamond ruler
- Additional straight ruler at least 18" long
- Black Sharpie marker
- Transparent packing tape

Work on a large flat surface such as a dining room table.

Jan's tip

This technique yields strips with bias edges. ALWAYS prepare the fabric in advance: Apply a mist of spray starch to the fabric. Press dry. For large yardage, mix liquid starch with water according to the manufacturer's directions. Spray with a mist bottle to moisten, or pour mixture in a container and saturate the fabric. Wring the fabric to remove most of the starch water. Press with a hot iron until dry.

1. Work on the bottom or printed side of a 6" or 6½" × 24" ruler. Align the centerline of the diamond ruler with the centerline of the long ruler. Draw against the edges of the diamond ruler, creating a 22.5° guideline on the straight ruler. Extend the line, using the extra ruler and drawing along the edge.

2. Rotate the diamond ruler, and repeat to create 2 intersecting 22.5° guidelines. Draw lines in this manner on the bottoms of both rulers.

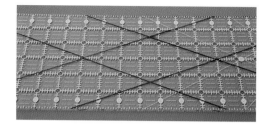

3. Tape the 2 long rulers end to end with transparent tape. Turn the taped double rulers right side up.

tape, 2 single-ended arrows

4. Cut the starched, pressed fabric yardage into 2 equal sections.

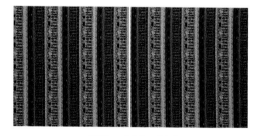

solid line dividing fabric

5. Place the fabrics on a large cutting mat, wrong sides together. Carefully align the stripes of both layers so they are on top of each other, regardless of any misalignment at the outer edges.

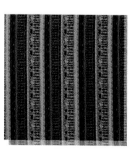

6. Place the long ruler across a corner of the fabric, and align the 22.5° guideline with a printed stripe. Cut through both layers along the edge of the ruler. When the fabric layers are separated, they will be mirror images.

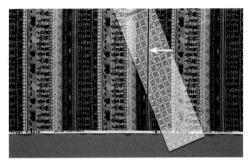

Placement for a right-handed cut

Placement for a left-handed cut

7. Cut strips at the correct width specified for your project. All strips will be slightly bias, and all will be angled strips.

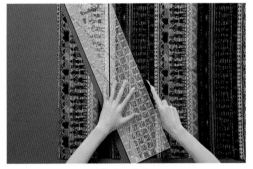

Right-handed cut

Left-handed cut

8. Following every cut, check the ruler alignment with the printed stripe. Make cleanup cuts as necessary to adjust the ruler alignment.

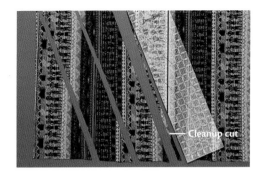

9. Continue cutting angled strips, edge to edge.

10. The angled strips may be cut into smaller sections with the full diamond or quarter- or half-diamond rulers. Construction details for the blocks used in *Dancing African Ladies* begin on page 70.

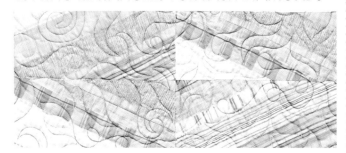

CUTTING RECTANGLES FOR FAUX DIAMONDS

Option 2: Allow the stripes to run in the same direction without matching the colors and direction, for a more random appearance.

Faux Diamonds are made from striped fabrics, but they're not really diamonds at all. This slick effect is created by strategically cutting striped fabrics with a rectangular ruler—no diamonds at all! For ease, select a cutting ruler with a 1-to-2 ratio, such as 4″ × 8″ or 6″ × 12″.

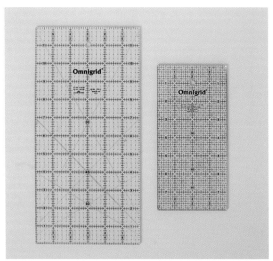

6″ × 12″ and 4″ × 8″ rectangular rulers with a 1-to-2 ratio

1. Starch the fabrics before cutting them, to stabilize the edges during construction.

2. Fold the fabric, wrong sides together, aligning the stripes.

Option 1: Align the stripes on both layers so they are running in the same direction, matching the same colors on the top and bottom layers.

3. Place the ruler on the fabric, aligning a stripe with the ¼″ seamline at opposite corners (the corners of the finished-size rectangle). The stripe should not bisect the outer corner of the ruler. Cut through the double thickness, creating rectangles with diagonal stripes.

- When you cut correctly, you should have equal numbers of mirror-image rectangles from the 2 layers.

- The final yield depends upon several factors: the amount of yardage available, the ruler size, and whether you are fussy cutting particular stripes or cutting randomly.

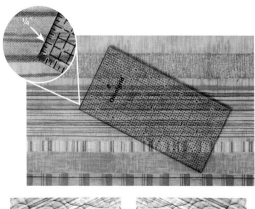

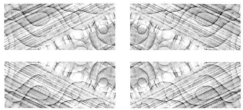

Equal quantities of mirror-image rectangles

Jan's tip

It is easier to match stripes that are very consistent! A printed stripe will typically have small irregularities, and may not match perfectly at the seams. This is normal but may not provide the appearance you desire. If the stripe is irregular, select an asymmetrical arrangement for greater success.

construction techniques

Many of the quilts included in this book are constructed in the same fashion. Therefore, general instructions will apply to the majority of the patterns, and specifics will appear in the instructions for each pattern.

Quick diamond quilts are quilts with rows of diamonds or partial diamond units in a variety of landscape or geometric designs. Many of the quilts incorporate clever cutting techniques using pieces from striped or strip-pieced fabrics—allowing you to create stunning designs easily while the fabric does the work!

Detail: Chevron Diamonds

Detail: Framed Diamonds

Diamond landscape

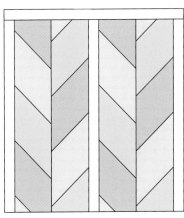

Diamond Braid

The designs in this book enable construction without any set-in seams. Two of the patterns spotlight machine appliqué embellishments for whimsical wall quilts.

Detail: Faux Diamonds

Detail: Super Scoops

Detail: Pretty Posies

Accuracy First

An accurate ¼″ seam is essential for making any quilt, but it is even more important when sewing quilts that include diamonds.

■ For best results, use a single-hole throat plate and a quarter-inch presser foot on your sewing machine.

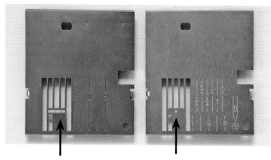

Standard throat plate (left); single-hole throat plate (right)

Examples of quarter-inch presser feet

■ Use a sharp machine needle (not universal or ballpoint). Set the stitch length to 1.5 or 2mm (12 to 15 stitches per inch).

■ Calibrate the seam allowance width before sewing your project! Accurate seam allowances are critical to the success of your quilt.

TEST FOR ACCURACY

1. Sew a seam test: Cut a 1½″-wide strip of fabric. Subcut into 6–9 sections.

2. Sew 3 pieces together along the long edges.

3. Press the seams open.

4. Measure the total width of the 3-strip sample. It should measure 3½″. If the strip sample is wider than 3½″, you need to make your seam 1 thread wider. If the strip sample is narrower than 3½″, you need to make your seam 1 thread narrower.

jan's tip

A handy tool is available to help you obtain an exact scant ¼″ seam allowance—the Perfect Piecing Seam Guide (see Resources, page 95). Lower the needle into the hole and lower the presser foot, keeping the tool parallel to the presser foot. Observe the right edge of the tool. Where is the perfect edge in relationship to the presser foot? For greater accuracy, create a raised guide on your machine bed, referring to Step 5, below.

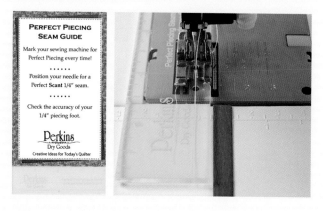

5. Once you have an accurate seam allowance, make a guide on your machine just ahead of and to the right of the presser foot. A guide can consist of any of the following:

■ A fine, permanent ink line on the bed of your machine

■ A stack of blue painter's tape (see Making a Tape Guide, page 17)

■ Adhesive-backed moleskin or dense foam (sold in the foot-care section of the pharmacy)

■ A commercial guide, available on some sewing machines

PRESSING MATTERS

Each of the quilt projects includes pressing instructions. For the greatest accuracy, press each seam after sewing it.

■ If the seams are to be pressed open, press from the wrong side, then inspect on the front.

■ If the seams are to be pressed to the side, press from the front, then inspect on the back.

■ Use your iron's shot-of-steam feature to flatten fabrics.

■ Use a mist of water before pressing if you do not have a shot-of-steam feature.

- Use a light mist of spray starch or fabric finish to provide body and prevent bias edges from stretching.

- After the quilt top is assembled, press with steam to flatten, smooth, and straighten the quilt top.

- Inspect the seams from the wrong side, pressing all the seams consistently in the same direction. Correct any seams that have accidentally twisted in the wrong direction, as this will be visible from the front of the quilt and may potentially affect the machine quilting results at the seam.

Jan's tip

Watch for pleats or folds at the seam when pressing. If the seam is not fully pressed, it changes the dimension of the quilt unit.

Mastering Angled Intersections

Angled intersections are beautiful when well executed, attesting to a quilter's expertise. There are several ways to sew diamond rows together. To achieve success with diamond designs, follow these important guidelines.

- Cut carefully. All diamond shapes must be true 45° angles (at the tips) and parallelograms (the same distance between straight edges in both directions).

- Maintain accurate seam allowances throughout construction. If time passes between the start and finish of a project, check your seam allowance when resuming the project. Sew with the same seam allowance as in the beginning.

- Control seam allowances in a neat manner to distribute bulk.

- Avoid rubbing the iron over the raised seams on the front, creating a "cooked" or shiny effect on the fabric.

Jan's tip

Pretrimming the points of the diamonds often helps align block pieces accurately. The partial diamond rulers and the template patterns in the book have angled corners to simplify alignment when piecing half diamonds together. Always trim any seam allowances (often called dog-ears) that extend beyond the diamonds after you have pieced them together.

SEWING DIAGONAL ROWS OF DIAMONDS

When stitching a diamond composition, you will arrange and sew the blocks in diagonal rows. The rows will be joined into larger sections—approximately the width of your ironing board—and then the sections will be joined to finish the quilt top.

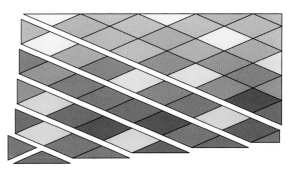

Diamonds are sewn in diagonal rows; partial diamonds finish the row ends.

Diamond rows may be offset to avoid matching seams and to create an organic flow for landscape designs. Trim the edges as needed.

Another option is to sew only whole diamonds together (omitting any partial diamonds in the corners and along the edges); offset the rows or match intersections as desired. After the rows are assembled and pressed, trim all 4 sides to straighten and square the edges.

Marking the ¼″ Intersections

Each of the quarter-, half-, and full diamond shapes has unique angles at the edges and tips, making assembly a bit challenging in the beginning.

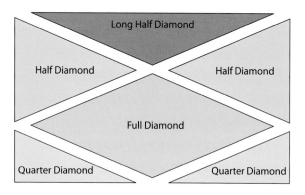

The quarter- and half-diamond rulers have small holes near the points, at the ¼″ seam intersections. If you make your own templates, I suggest making a small hole at the seam intersections. Use a fine, sharp pencil or textile pen to mark through the holes on the *wrong side* of the fabric to assist in aligning the pieces when pinning.

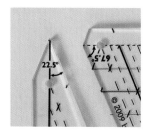 

Holes at the ¼″ seam intersections allow for precision marking to help align pieces for pinning.

Mark the ¼″ seam intersection with a dot on the wrong side of the fabric.

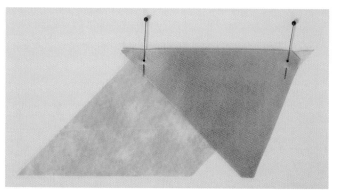

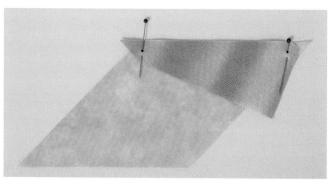

Align the pencil dots to accurately pin the diamond to adjacent pieces.

When piecing a large number of the same shapes, you will become skilled at gauging the alignment at both ends and will sew accurately without marking the dots. Your goal: accurate rows with straight outside edges.

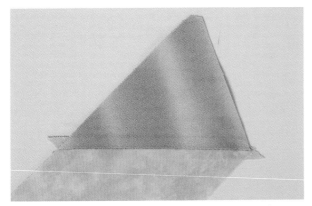

Front view of a diamond and half diamond pieced together

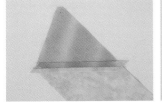

Press the seams open or to the side.

jan's tip

You will need a variety of marking pencils for visibility on light, medium, dark, and patterned fabrics. Use the minimal amount of ink or pencil lead necessary to see the small dot—otherwise the mark may be visible on the front of the quilt!

Sewing Rows of Diamonds Together

1. Insert a pin vertically between 2 diamond rows, matching the pencil marks to align intersections. Keep this pin perpendicular to the fabric.

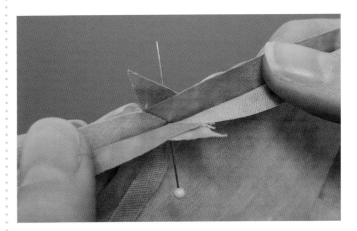

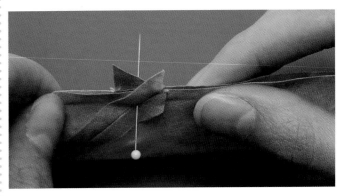

2. Secure the intersection with a second pin inserted at a shallow angle. (Do not tilt and anchor the first pin, as it will slide the 2 layers apart, resulting in a mismatched intersection.) Typically, the 2 quarter-inch tips overlap, approximately ⅛″ at the base. Maintain this proportion as the 2 seams overlap, and the seam allowances will match when sewn.

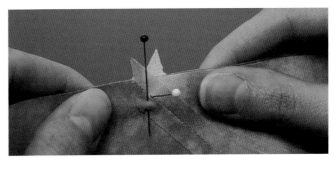

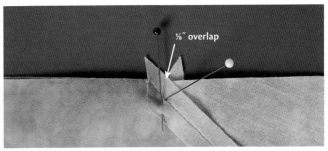

⅛″ overlap

3. Remove only the vertical pin, and sew the seam. You should still have the ⅛″ overlap. When the seams match perfectly on the front, they will appear slightly mismatched when looking at the opened seam on the wrong side.

The ⅛″ offset is due to the angle of the diamonds.

Points are perfectly matched on the front.

Points appear slightly mismatched when seams are pressed open, on the wrong side.

Jan's tip

This overlap seam-alignment technique works only when the seam allowances are pressed *open*.

Sewing Half-Diamond Units

Several quilt designs are constructed with half diamonds, also known as isosceles triangles. These triangles have two sides of equal length. Two half diamonds, sewn together along the short edges, create a complete 45° diamond. These patterns include Thousand Pyramids, Framed Diamonds, and Chevron Diamonds.

Thousand Pyramids variation

Framed Diamonds

Chevron Diamonds

THOUSAND PYRAMIDS TECHNIQUE

Arrange the triangles on the design wall, moving fabrics around until you are satisfied with the color placement. Combine larger and smaller triangles together for more interest. Sew the smaller half diamonds together first. Give this clever technique a try.

1. Arrange the 4 triangles to be sewn together.

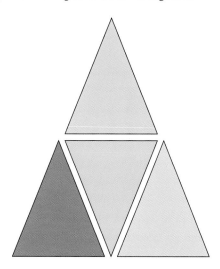

2. Flip the top triangle right sides together with the bottom center triangle.

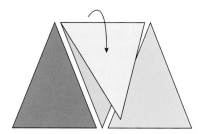

3. Sew the seam between the 2 triangles.

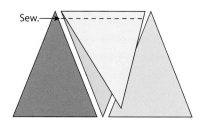

4. Move the unit about 1" out from the presser foot, and finger-press the seam open. Do not cut the thread. Position the unit right side up, ready to add the next triangle.

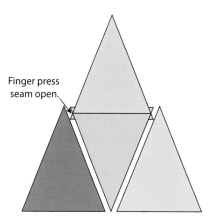

Finger press seam open.

5. Flip the third triangle onto the first 2 triangles. Sew the seam. Again move the unit about 1" away from the presser foot without cutting the thread. Finger-press the second seam open.

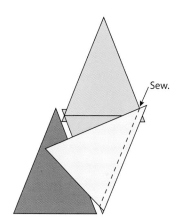

Sew.

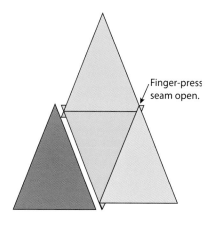

Finger-press seam open.

6. Position the fourth triangle and sew the final seam. Press with a hot iron.

Half-diamond triangles (or triangle units, as in Thousand Pyramids) may be assembled into rows 3 different ways:

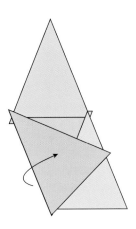

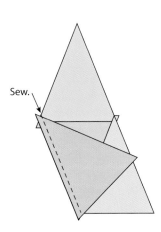

Sew.

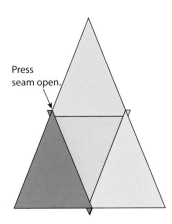

Press seam open.

Traditional setting of horizontal rows, mirrored effect

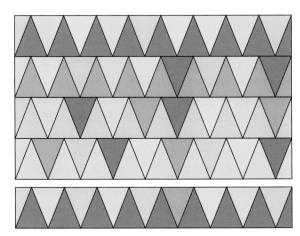

Zigzag or "shark's teeth" effect

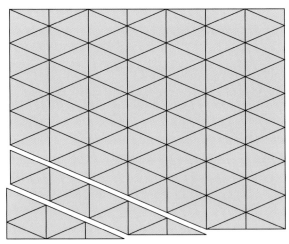

Diagonal rows of half diamonds for chevron patterns

STRIP-PIECING FRAMED DIAMONDS

When constructing the *Dancing African Ladies* Framed Diamonds quilt, I developed an interesting method of construction.

1. Apply a mist of spray starch to the fabric before cutting. Cut 2 layers, wrong sides together, creating mirror-image angled strips. See Cutting Angled Strips for Framed Diamonds, page 20. Cut strips 4½" wide for the 6½" half diamond.

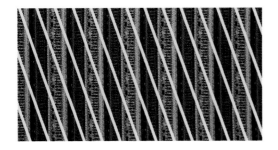

2. Arrange mirrored strips side by side in pairs, matching the stripe pattern. Align the strips with right sides together. Sew a seam, joining pairs of strips.

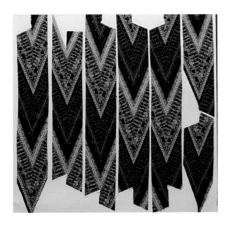

3. Cut several half diamonds from the angled strip set using the fast2cut half-diamond ruler or a template made from the the half-diamond pattern on pullout page P2. Align the centerline of the ruler or template with the center seam.

jan's tip

For greater interest, select different areas of the fabric print to take advantage of all the color changes and patterns in the striped fabric.

4. Apply double-stick tape to the center seam of the cut half-diamond at both ends; this will keep the fabrics from shifting while you cut the matching half diamonds in the next steps.

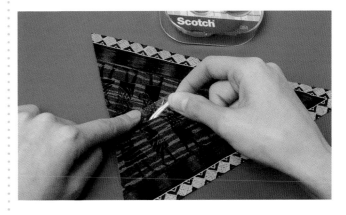

5. Position the half diamonds along the remaining pieced strips to locate a mate for each.

6. Place the ruler or template on top and cut a matching half diamond for each piece.

7. Align pairs of half diamonds, and sew the center seams. Due to irregularities in printing, the print may not match perfectly, but this will not affect the quilt top. Press with a light mist of water to reactivate the spray starch in the fabric. Sew scraps together to create additional units if desired.

Borders

The quilt patterns and gallery quilts in this book feature a variety of borders. While I have no particular border formula, I do have some favorite combinations.

- Spacer strip border: Add a narrow border 1″–3″ wide using fabric that contrasts or coordinates with the center of the quilt. This narrow border provides visual space between the center of the quilt and the outer borders.

- Double border: Add 2 fabric strips of different widths.

- Triple border: Add 3 fabric strips of different widths.

- Accent trim: Include a narrow contrasting trim strip.

- Combination borders: Add strips of varying widths, plus an accent trim strip.

- Bias-cut striped border: Cut stripes on the bias. For stability, add lightweight fusible interfacing to the back of the fabric before sewing it to the quilt top. Mitered corners are recommended.

- Striped border: Cut border strips perpendicular to the stripe for a dramatic color effect.

- Preprinted border strips: Use fabrics that are specially printed in linear bands for borders.

jan's tip

When possible, cut the borders parallel to the selvage before cutting the other components of the quilt. The lengthwise grain is the most stable and will minimize waviness and rippling in the borders. Typically, cutting lengthwise requires more yardage to create a continuous border.

If you have less yardage to work with, or the printed pattern works better in sections, cut the border strips in shorter lengths, either lengthwise or cross grain, and sew the strips end to end. Use a walking foot to prevent the upper layer of fabric from stretching when you are sewing the strips together.

Do not add the borders without measuring the quilt top first. Always mark opposing borders, and pin the borders to the top on a flat surface. This takes a few extra minutes, but it will ensure that the borders will fit the quilt top accurately, providing a polished finish without ruffling at the edge of the quilt. Use a walking foot when sewing and adding borders to avoid stretching one or more of the layers.

BORDERS WITH BUTTED CORNERS

The simplest and most straightforward borders are applied directly to the quilt top—a border-as-you-go process. Work on a large, flat surface such as a dining room table or kitchen counter to keep the quilt top flat and straight. Use a dressmaker's measuring tape or a carpenter's retractable ruler.

1. Measure the length of the quilt top through the center and in several other places. (Do not use the outer side measurements, as the edges can be stretched from handling.) Find the average of these measurements, and cut 2 side borders to this length.

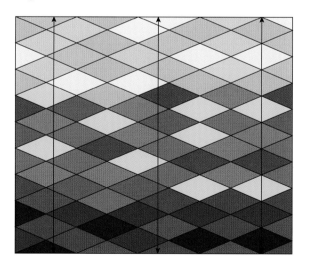

2. Fold both borders in half, bringing the short edges together to find the center. Mark each center fold with a pin or a light pencil mark.

3. Place the quilt top right side up on a flat, smooth surface. Place 1 border right side down along the quilt edge, matching the center points. Pin in the center and at both ends. Pin approximately every 3"–4" along the length. Pin the second border to the opposite side in the same manner.

4. Sew the first 2 borders to the quilt top. Press the seams toward the border.

5. Measure the width of the quilt top through the center in several places, including the borders just added. Find the average of these measurements, and cut 2 strips of the border fabric this length for the top and bottom. Mark the center points as before, and pin the border strips to the top and bottom of the quilt, matching the centers and ends. Sew, and press the seams toward the border.

6. Continue adding borders in the same manner—measuring the quilt and cutting and adding borders—until the quilt top reaches the desired size or until the border width visually balances the quilt center. Press the seams outward for all borders.

MITERED BORDERS

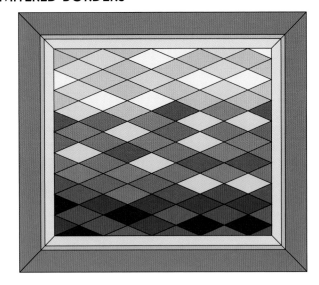

Mitered borders are attractive on diamond quilts. They are not difficult to sew when you know the secrets! Mitered borders are versatile and polished and may be used on any quilt style. When adding more than one border, sew the border strips together first along their long edges, and press; then add them to the quilt top as one unit. The project cutting instructions will tell you how long to cut the border strips.

1. Cut strips as directed, or as desired, to create the borders for your quilt. Audition the border strips by pinning them around the quilt top on the design wall and viewing the effect from a distance. The strips will be several inches wider and longer than the quilt top. Note that the innermost borders do not need to be as long as the outer borders.

2. Once you are satisfied with the combination of the various fabrics and strip widths, sew the border strips together, matching the centers. Create 4 border units keeping the order of the strips the same in each. Press the seams of the top and bottom border units *toward the outer border*. Press the seams of the side border units *toward the inner border*. This will allow the seams at the corners to butt together for easier matching when you miter the corners later. Skip this step if you are adding only a single mitered border.

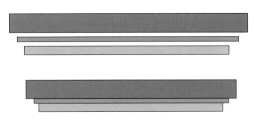

Make 4.

Cutting for Mitered Borders

To calculate the lengths to cut mitered borders for any quilt, follow these steps:

1. *Measure several places across the width of the quilt. Do not measure the outer edges, as they may have stretched. Find the average of these measurements, and write it down. Do the same for the length, and write the measurement down.*

2. *Measure the width of the border or border unit that you will be adding. Multiply this measurement by 2.*

3. *Add the result of Step 2 to the width and length from Step 1. Then add an extra 4". This is how long the border strips should be. You will need the extra length so that you can easily sew the diagonal seams at the corners.*

Formula:

Quilt width or length

+ (2 × border width)

+ 4"
_____

Total = Length to cut borders

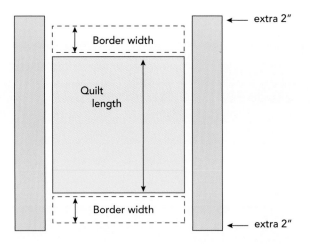

3. Fold each border to find the center. Mark with a pin or a pencil mark. From the center, measure out *half* the width or length of the quilt, and make a mark on each end. This is the point that you will align with the corner of the quilt top.

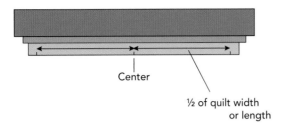

Center

½ of quilt width or length

4. Fold and mark the center point on all 4 edges of the quilt top with a pin or light pencil mark. Mark the end of the seam ¼" from the raw edge at all 4 corners.

5. Place the quilt top face up on a flat surface. Place a border on the quilt top, right sides together, aligning the inner-border raw edges with the quilt-top raw edges.

6. Align the center and end points, and pin the border to the quilt top. Pin approximately 4"–5" apart, easing fullness along the edges as necessary. Repeat on the opposing side, pinning the second border in place.

7. With the wrong side of the quilt on top, sew the border to the quilt top, beginning ¼" from the raw edge. Take 2 or 3 stitches, and then backstitch to secure the end of the seam. Sew the seam, stopping and backstitching ¼" from the edge. Press the seams outward.

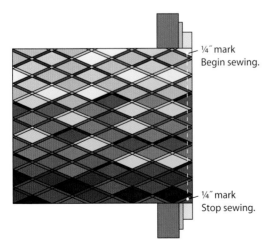

¼" mark Begin sewing.

¼" mark Stop sewing.

jan's tip

If your sewing table is small, extend the surface area by placing an ironing board next to the sewing table; adjust the board to a compatible height.

8. Repeat the process to sew the 2 remaining borders to the quilt top. The borders will extend beyond the quilt top at all the corners.

9. Fold the quilt diagonally, wrong sides together, aligning adjacent borders on top of each other. If necessary, fold back the pressed seam allowance, exposing the stitching line between the quilt top and the border.

10. Position the fast2cut 45° diamond ruler with one edge against the stitching line and the 135° corner at the end of the stitching line.

11. Mark a light, visible stitching line for the mitered border from the previous stitching to the outer edges of the border at a 135° angle.

12. Pin the 2 border strips together along the marked line to hold them together for sewing. Sew the seam, beginning at the previous ¼" seam, backstitching and sewing to the outer edge of the border. Remove each pin as you sew. Backstitch.

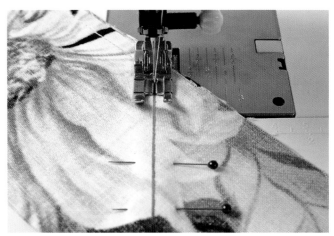

13. Open the quilt top. Press the corner neatly. Visually examine the corner to verify that it lies perfectly flat without puckers or bulges. If necessary, adjust by removing and re-stitching the seam to achieve a perfect corner.

14. Once you are satisfied with the seam, trim the excess border fabric, leaving a ¼" seam allowance. Repeat the process for all 4 corners, and press the seams open.

Adding Narrow Accent Trim to Mitered Borders

1. Cut 4 strips 1″ wide of the same length as the corresponding borders or as directed by the project instructions. Place 1 contrasting trim strip, right sides together, aligned with the edge of 1 border strip; match the center of the long edges of the accent trim strip with the center of the border strip.

2. Sew, stitching ½″ from the raw edges, down the center of the trim strip. Cut away excess seam allowance of the trim strip only between the stitching and the raw edges (known as "grading the seam") to remove bulk.

3. Press the accent trim strip to cover the stitching. The raw edges should be aligned.

4. Repeat for all 4 borders.

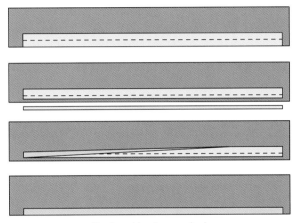

Border with trim attached

Finishing Notes

Once your quilt top is complete, you're ready to move on to layering, basting, quilting, and binding. There isn't space to cover all those details in this book. If you need additional information, check out some of the many good books on basic quiltmaking.

The backing yardage allows for a backing that is 6″ to 8″ larger than the quilt top. If you want to add a hanging sleeve that matches the backing, purchase an extra ¼–½ yard. For these quick diamond quilts, I cut binding strips 2¾″ wide. I like the look of a wider binding with the larger-scale blocks. Feel free to cut narrower binding strips if you prefer.

ADDING A HANGING SLEEVE

I like to add a sleeve before the binding is sewn on. Here's my special way of making a full sleeve that will not create a rod-shaped lump on the front of the quilt.

1. Cut a piece of fabric that is 9″ × the width of your quilt. Turn the short edges under ¼″ to ½″ twice and hem both 9″ ends by machine.

2. Fold the fabric lengthwise, wrong sides together, with approximately ⅓ of the top right side visible. Machine baste a line of stitching ½″ from the fold; this will create a pleat.

3. Fold the pleated sleeve fabric in half lengthwise, aligning both raw edges with the quilt top on the back. The pleat is on the outside or top layer. Center and pin the sleeve along the top edges to secure.

4. Sew the binding to the upper edge of the quilt, simultaneously catching the raw edges of the sleeve. Fold the binding over, encasing the quilt and sleeve edges. Sew the final edges of the binding and the sleeve to the quilt back by hand.

5. Remove the basting stitches. The sleeve now has approximately 1″ of fullness on the back. When a hanging rod is inserted in the sleeve, the front of the quilt will hang straight and flat.

diamond gallery

Carnival, Thousand Pyramids Faux Diamond wallhanging,
32½″ × 62½″, 2007, by Jan Krentz; machine quilting by Sue Mezera, Poway, CA

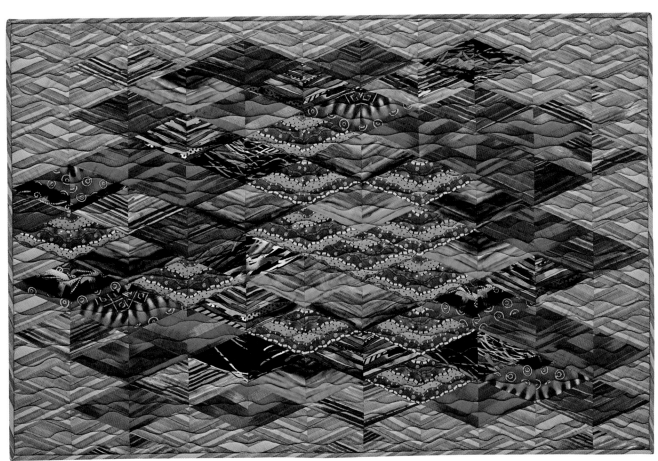

Luminescence, Quick Chevron landscape wallhanging (4½″ diamonds), 44½″ × 29″, 2008,
by Jan Krentz; machine quilting by Janet Sturdevant Stuart, Fort Worth, TX

Aztec Poppies, diamond landscape quilt, 98″ × 95″, 2008,
by Jan Krentz; machine quilting by Janet Sturdevant Stuart, Fort Worth, TX

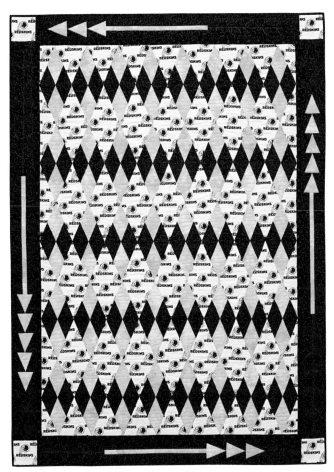

For My Redskin Fan, diamond landscape variation,
52" × 73½", 2008, by Kathy Butler, Philomath, OR;
machine quilting by Jill Miller, Corvallis, OR

Oriental Masketry, Framed Diamond table topper, 24" × 40", 2008,
by Betty Alofs, Lakeside, CA

Flight of the Butterfly, original 3-D Diamond variation wallhanging, 24″ × 37″, 2004, by Jan Darnell, Taylorsville, KY

Dollie's Quilt, diamond landscape variation with 1930s Sunbonnet
Sue appliqués, 60″ × 92″, 2008, by Carol Gilbert, Poway, CA;
machine quilting by Lois Russell, San Diego, CA

Loves It, diamond rag quilt variation, 47″ × 65″, 2009,
by Cindy Stearns, Fallbrook, CA

Rejoice, diamond landscape with appliqué, 26″ × 33″, 2009,
by Cindy Stearns, Fallbrook, CA

Decorated Diamonds, original diamond wallhanging, 40″ × 40″, 2009,
by Jacqueline Hand Lacey, Encinitas, CA

The Kalahari Desert in Bloom, Framed Diamond variation, 47½″ × 56″, 2007, by Pat Wolfe, San Diego, CA

Cornfields, Diamond Braid variation with appliqué, 24″ × 30½″, 2009, by Patricia Votruba, San Diego, CA

Hollyhock Garden, diamond landscape variation with appliqué, 31½″ × 58″, 2009, by Patricia Votruba, San Diego, CA

Sherbet for the Girls, Faux Diamond baby quilt, 36¾″ × 49″, 2007, by Allegra "Lee" Olson, San Diego, CA

Blueberry Parfait, Framed Diamond wallhanging, 36½″ × 35¾″, 2007,
by Allegra "Lee" Olson, San Diego, CA

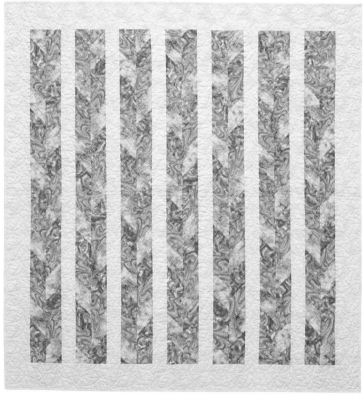

Beach Blanket Braid, 3″ Diamond Braid quilt, 64″ × 68″, 2007,
by Amy Wazny, San Diego, CA; machine quilting
by Marita Wallace, Santee, CA

Bahama Breeze, Chevron Diamond quilt with appliqué, 65½" × 52¼", 2007, by Allegra "Lee" Olson, San Diego, CA

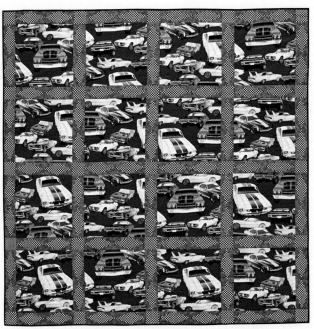

Road Trip, diamond sashing quilt, 66" × 66", 2008, by Kathy Butler, Philomath, OR

Aloha Christmas, original diamond landscape variation, 33" × 23½", 2007, by Suzanne Muse Taylor, Escondido, CA

The Gardener's Friend, Faux Diamond wallhanging with appliqué, 40" × 30", 2009, by Kathy Butler, Philomath, OR

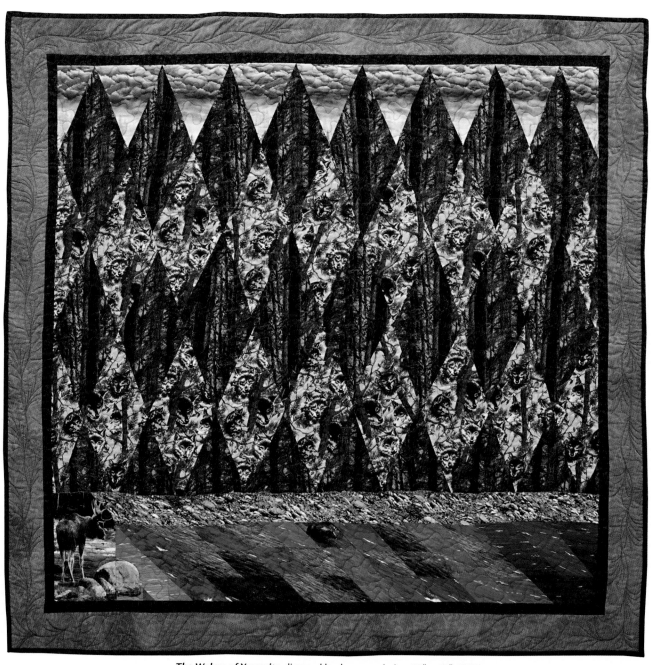

The Wolves of Yosemite, diamond landscape variation, 59″ × 57″, 2007,
by Anna Mae Bach, San Diego, CA; machine quilting by Lois Russell, San Diego, CA

Dangling Shells,
diamond purse, 10″ × 11″, 2007,
by Betty Alofs, Lakeside, CA

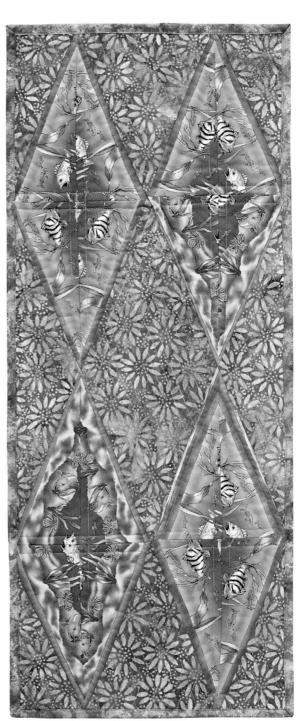

Paddington's Pleasures, Framed Diamond quilt, 52″ × 63″, 2007,
by Nancy Rowland, Palmer, AK

Fishin' for Diamonds, Framed Diamond table topper, 13″ × 31″,
2008, by Betty Alofs, Lakeside, CA

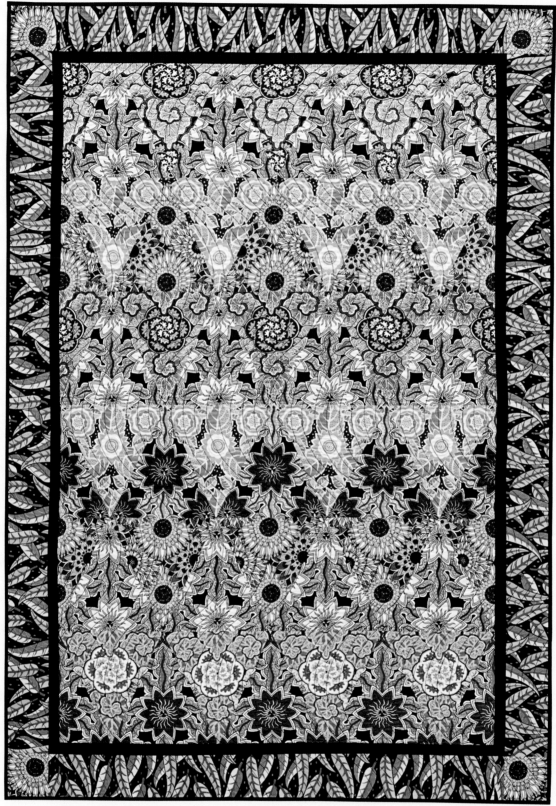

Exotic Garden Kaleidoscope, Thousand Pyramids quilt, 50" × 70", 2003, by Jane Sassaman, Harvard, IL

Floral Fantasy Kaleidoscope, Thousand Pyramids quilt, 50″ × 70″, 2004,
by Jane Sassaman, Harvard, IL

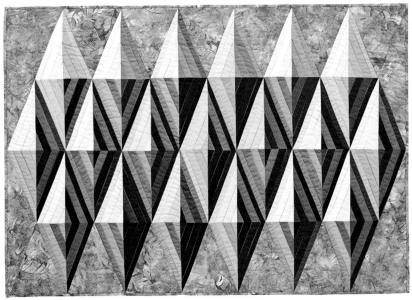

Color Stripes, 3-D Diamond quilt, 30¾″ × 45″, 2007, by Julia Zgliniec, Poway, CA

Wing Dings, original 3-D Diamond variation quilt, 57″ × 47″, 2001,
by Frances Cunningham, Santa Cruz, CA; machine quilting by Faye Collinsworth, Dublin, CA

Halloween Dance, Framed Diamond quilt, 97″ × 102″, 2008,
by B.J. Coopes, Anchorage, AK

Garden in the Wood, Diamond Braid quilt, 69″ × 94″, 2007,
by B.J. Coopes, Anchorage, AK; from the collection
of Cathy Dimaria, Anchorage, AK

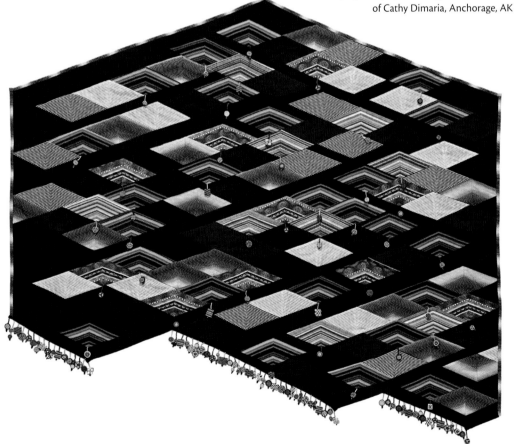

Bejeweled, original diamond landscape variation, 43″ × 38″, 2008, by Suzanne Muse Taylor, Escondido, CA

■ fast2cut Fussy Cutter 45° diamond ruler 3″; or 3″ diamond template pattern (pullout page P2)

Skill level: Advanced beginner

Finished Block size: 2½″ diamond

DISTANT HORIZON

39″ × 33″, 2006, by Jan Krentz

I created this calm landscape quilt with a collection of Timeless Treasures fabrics. You can use both right and wrong sides of the fabric to increase the number of color values, tints, and shades. I combined 3″ diamonds and pieced four-patch diamonds (made of 1³/₄″ diamonds) for more interest. Select a collection of scraps, fat eighths, and fat quarters to create your own impressionist landscape!

Fabric Requirements and Cutting

Refer to Prewashing Guidelines on page 9 to determine whether to wash your fabrics before cutting and sewing. See Cutting Techniques, beginning on page 11, for details on cutting methods as needed. Cut a variety of diamonds from each value; the numbers of diamonds to cut are approximate.

YARDAGE	FOR	CUTTING
⅞ to 1 yard total light-value fabrics in soft blue, aqua, teal, yellow, and peach	Diamonds	Cut 48 diamonds, 2″.
		Cut 60 diamonds, 3″.
⅔ to ¾ yard total medium-value fabrics in blue, teal, and green	Diamonds	Cut 35 diamonds, 2″.
		Cut 50 diamonds, 3″.
⅝ to ¾ yard total dark-value fabrics in teal, navy blue, green, brown, and black	Diamonds	Cut 30 diamonds, 2″.
		Cut 40 diamonds, 3″.
¼ yard each of 1 light and 1 dark print	Binding	Cut 2 strips, 2¾″ × 42″, from each to total 160″.
1½ yards fabric	Backing	

Batting: 45″ × 39″

Quilt Assembly

Be sure to read Construction Techniques, beginning on page 23, before beginning your project.

Jan's tip

The smaller diamonds for the four-patch units were cut slightly oversized, at 2″. To create the 1¾″ diamond four-patch units, you will piece 4 small diamonds together, then press and trim to 3″.

1. Arrange the diamonds on the design wall. Move the pieces around to create a landscape-effect composition. The four-patch units will be interchangeable in size with the 3″ diamonds. Use the quilt diagram below as a guide for placing the diamonds. Note that I arranged the diamond rows so that they are offset in my quilt.

2. When you are happy with the arrangement, sew the smaller diamonds into diamond four-patch units, and trim, using the 3″ diamond ruler. Be sure the center seam intersection is centered in the diamond.

3. Sew diagonal diamond rows, either matching the intersections or offsetting the units in a brick pattern.

4. Press the quilt top thoroughly. Trim with a rotary cutter and ruler to straighten the edges and square the corners.

5. Layer the quilt top with the batting and backing, and baste. Quilt as desired. Bind.

Quilt diagram

- Quick Diamond Braid
- fast2cut Fussy Cutter 45° diamond ruler 6½"; or 6½" diamond template pattern (pullout page P2)

Skill level: Skilled beginner

Finished Block size: 6" diamond

HAPPY DAYS

62" × 71", 2007, by Jan Krentz; machine quilting by Sue Mezera, Poway, CA

This happy quilt is reminiscent of Grandmother's braided rugs. Each Diamond Braid is a column of three fabrics. The diamonds are cut with two sides on grain and two sides true bias. The quilt also features a drop shadow behind each braid. Colorful fabrics guarantee that this quilt will become a favorite!

Fabric Requirements and Cutting

Refer to Prewashing Guidelines on page 9 to determine whether to wash your fabrics before cutting and sewing. See Cutting Techniques, beginning on page 11, for details, and use the strip method of cutting diamonds. Layer the 6½" strips wrong sides together in pairs to cut the diamonds.

YARDAGE	FOR	CUTTING
½ yard each of 4 different yellow fabrics	Diamonds	Cut 2 strips, 6½" × 42", from each; layer and cut 6 diamonds, 6½" (3 angled right and 3 angled left), from each (24 total).
½ yard each of 4 different pink fabrics	Diamonds	Cut 2 strips, 6½" × 42", from each; layer and cut 6 diamonds, 6½" (3 angled right and 3 angled left), from each (24 total).
½ yard each of 4 different blue fabrics	Diamonds	Cut 2 strips, 6½" × 42", from each; layer and cut 6 diamonds, 6½" (3 angled right and 3 angled left), from each (24 total).
½ yard dark blue or gray fabric	Drop-shadow sashing	Cut 7 strips, 1½" × 42". Cut 4 strips, 1½" × 13".
2 yards* white print fabric	Sashing and borders	Cut 8 squares, 1½" × 1½". Cut 3 strips, 2½" × 67½", for sashing. Cut 2 strips, 2½" × 67½", for side borders. Cut 2 strips, 2½" × 62½", for top and bottom borders.
⅝ yard fabric	Binding	Cut 7 strips, 2¾" × 42".
4½ yards fabric	Backing	
Batting: 70" × 79"		

*If you don't mind piecing the sashing and borders, 1 yard is enough.

Quilt Assembly

Be sure to read Construction Techniques, beginning on page 23, before beginning your project.

1. Choose a yellow, pink, and blue for each vertical row, and arrange the diamonds on the design wall. Alternate the 3 colors within each row as shown in the photo (page 56) and quilt diagram (page 58). Arrange the straight-grain edges so they are parallel with the outside edges of the quilt. Make 2 vertical rows of 9 diamonds each using 3 of the fabrics. Repeat with the other color combinations to create 2 vertical rows for each of the 4 braids (8 rows total).

2. Sew the diamonds into rows, and press. Then sew the vertical seam between 2 matching diamond rows, offsetting the horizontal seams by about 4¼" to create a braided effect. Press each row, and trim each row to 66½" long.

3. Sew a 1½" square cut from white print sashing fabric to one end of each 67½" shadow strip. Position the shadow strip and square unit right sides together and long edges aligned with a Diamond Braid, aligning the square with the upper right corner of the Diamond Braid. Sew, trim even with the braid, and press the seams toward the braid. Repeat for the remaining 3 braids.

4. Sew a white print 1½" square to one end of each 1½" × 13" shadow strip. Position the shadow strip right sides together along the bottom of a Diamond Braid, aligning the square with the lower left corner of the Diamond Braid. Sew, trim even with the braid, and press the seams toward the braid. Repeat for the remaining 3 braids.

5. Sew a white print sashing strip to the right edge of each of 3 Diamond Braid units (the sashing is sewn to the drop shadow edge). Trim even with the braid. Press toward the sashing.

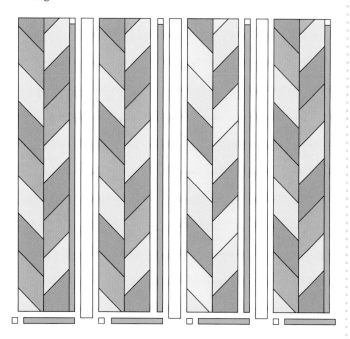

6. Join the 4 braids side by side, with the sashing strips between to make the center panel. Press.

7. Sew 2 outer borders to the right and left edges of the center panel. Press. Sew the remaining 2 borders to the top and bottom of the center panel. Trim even with the previous borders, and press.

8. Layer the quilt top with the batting and backing, and baste. Quilt as desired. Bind.

Quilt diagram

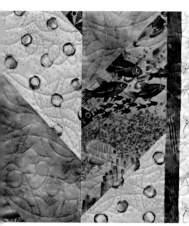

- Quick Chevron Diamonds
- fast2cut Fussy Cutter half-diamond ruler 6½" and fast2cut quarter-diamond ruler 6½"; or 6½" half-diamond template pattern and 6½" quarter-diamond template pattern (pullout page P2)

Skill level: Advanced beginner

Finished Block size: 6" half diamond

HIDDEN PATH

45½" × 32", 2008, by Jan Krentz; machine quilting by Janet Sturdevant Stuart, Fort Worth, TX

Hidden Path is a simple Chevron Diamond design with a contemporary graphic appearance. I used a printed stripe with varying-width color bands. This design may also be created from pieced strip-sets with fabrics from your collection.

Fabric Requirements and Cutting

Refer to Prewashing Guidelines on page 9 to determine whether to wash your fabrics before cutting and sewing. See Cutting Half-Diamonds, beginning on page 15, for details on cutting stripes and mirror-image designs as needed. Use the same method for the quarter diamonds along the bottom. For the quarter diamonds across the top, align the two narrow points of the quarter-diamond ruler with the cut edges of the strips so that the stripe bisects the right angle of the ruler.

YARDAGE	FOR	CUTTING
2½ yards striped fabric	Half and quarter diamonds	Cut 36 half diamonds, 6½" (18 angled right, 18 angled left)—1 is extra.
		Cut 12 quarter diamonds (6 angled right, 6 angled left)—2 are extra.
¼ yard gold fabric	Accent trim	Cut 2 strips, 1" × 32".
		Cut 2 strips, 1" × 42".
1½ yards green fabric*	Border	Cut 2 strips, 3½" × 38", on the lengthwise grain.
		Cut 2 strips, 3½" × 50", on the lengthwise grain.
½ yard fabric	Binding	Cut 5 strips, 2¾" × 42".
1⅝ yards fabric	Backing	
Batting: 52" × 38"		

*If you prefer to cut the border strips crosswise and piece them, ⅔ yard is enough.

Quilt Assembly

Be sure to read Construction Techniques, beginning on page 23, before beginning your project.

1. Arrange all the cut pieces on the design wall, orienting the half diamonds so the stripe parallels the top edge of each piece. Match the stripes to create mirror-image chevron patterns, or arrange them more randomly for an asymmetrical, abstract appearance, as I did.

2. Sew the half-diamond triangles together to create the 5 vertical rows. Pay attention to the placement of the stripe pattern. Add quarter-diamond pieces to the top and bottom of each row. Sew the rows together and press seam allowances as you go.

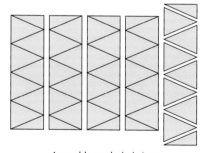

Assembly, exploded view

3. Refer to Mitered Borders, page 34, and Adding Narrow Accent Trim to Mitered Borders, page 37, to make the border units using the 1" gold accent strips and the 3½" green strips. Sew the borders to the quilt. Press.

4. Layer the quilt top with the batting and backing, and baste. Quilt as desired. Bind.

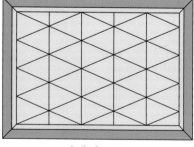

Quilt diagram

- Quick Chevron Diamonds with appliqué

- fast2cut Fussy Cutter half-diamond ruler 6½″ and quarter-diamond ruler 6½″; or 6½″ half-diamond template pattern and 6½″ quarter-diamond template pattern (pullout page P2)

Skill level: Advanced beginner or intermediate

Finished Block size: 6″ diamond

PRETTY POSIES

39″ × 39″, 2008, by Jan Krentz; machine quilting by Janet Sturdevant Stuart, Fort Worth, TX

Create a quick and easy background from chevron half diamonds, and embellish it with sunny, whimsical flowers, a dragonfly, and a hummingbird. This cheerful quilt will provide the joy of spring all year round!

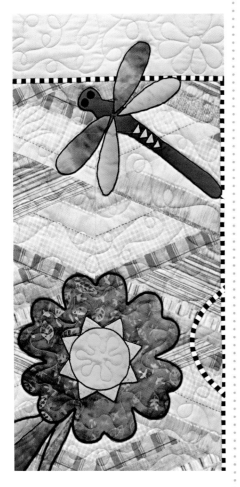

Fabric Requirements and Cutting

Refer to Prewashing Guidelines on page 9 to determine whether to wash your fabrics before cutting and sewing. See Cutting Half Diamonds, beginning on page 15, for details on cutting stripes and mirror-image designs as needed. Repeat the process for the quarter diamonds.

YARDAGE	FOR	CUTTING
2½ yards pastel stripe	Pieced background	Cut 36 half diamonds, 6½″ (18 angled right, 18 angled left). Cut 8 quarter diamonds, 6½″ (4 angled right, 4 angled left).
¼ yard black-and-white stripe	Narrow accent trim and dragonfly flight path	Cut 4 strips, 1″ × 42″. Cut 1 strip, ¾″ × 42″.
⅔ yard multicolored pastel fabric*	Border	Cut 4 strips, 4½″ × 42″.
¾ yard total of green fabrics	Stems and leaves	Cut 3 stems and 4 split leaves using the patterns on pullout page P2.
¾ yard total of assorted bright-colored fabrics in pink, red, orange, light green, yellow-gold, teal, blue, and black	Flowers, bird, and dragonfly	Cut the appliqué shapes for the bird, flowers, and dragonfly using the patterns on pullout page P2.
½ yard fabric	Binding	Cut 5 strips 2¾″ × 42″.
2½ yards fabric	Backing	
2 yards 18″-wide paper-backed fusible web	Appliqué	
5 yards 18″-wide tear-away stabilizer	Appliqué	
1 skein each of assorted colors of craft cord and matching thread OR 1–3 skeins black cording and black thread	Couching around appliqués (optional)	
Batting: 45″ × 45″		

*Note: Your fabric must be at least 42″ wide after removing the selvages, or you will need to piece the border strips. For lengthwise cutting, purchase 1¼ yards.

Background Assembly

Be sure to read Construction Techniques, beginning on page 23, before beginning your project.

1. Sew half diamonds together to create 14 Chevron Diamonds for the background.

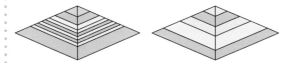

2. Arrange the 14 diamonds horizontally in rows, with the points touching, on the design wall. Refer to the diagram on page 63.

3. Sew 2 pairs of quarter diamonds together, and place them at the center top and bottom of the quilt. Fill in each corner with a quarter diamond, and the rest of the side edges with the remaining half diamonds.

4. Sew the pieces into diagonal rows. See Sewing Diagonal Rows of Diamonds, page 25. Sew the rows together to create the quilt top. Spray the top with spray starch. Press the seams neatly.

5. Trim with a rotary cutter and ruler to straighten the quilt top. I trimmed about ¾" off the top and bottom edges to make the center of the quilt square.

6. Refer to Mitered Borders, page 34, and Adding Narrow Trim Strips to Mitered Borders, page 37, to make border units using the 1" black-and-white strips and the 4½" pastel border strips. Sew the border units to the quilt.

Chevron Diamond quilt top, ready for appliqué embellishment

Appliqué Embellishment

PREPARE THE APPLIQUÉS

1. Trace the design shapes for all the leaves, stems, flowers, and other elements on the paper side of a lightweight iron-on fusible web adhesive product. The pattern should be a reverse image of the finished design.

2. Number or identify each shape, including the color or fabric to be used. Write this information close to and inside the drawn lines.

3. Roughly cut out the traced shapes, leaving a ¼" to ½" margin around each shape. For the larger shapes (such as the leaves, flowers, circles, dragonfly wings, and body), fold each shape, and snip about ¼" inside the traced line to create a small opening for the scissors. Unfold the shape and cut away the interior fusible web, leaving approximately ¼" inside the traced line. Use the trimmings for smaller appliqué shapes.

Trace the shapes onto fusible web.

Roughly cut out the traced shapes.

Jan's tip

For larger shapes, cut away the inner portion of the shape, leaving a ¼″ margin of fusible web just inside the drawn outline. This allows the final shape to remain soft and pliable, with fusible adhesive only along the margin of the piece.

4. Iron each fusible pattern piece to the wrong side of the corresponding fabric.

5. Cut out each design element on the line with sharp fabric scissors.

6. Turn under the raw edges of the ¾″ × 42″ strip of black-and-white stripe ¼″, and press, creating a strip about ¼″ wide for the dragonfly's flight path.

Jan's tip

For less confusion, keep each motif with all its components in a separate ziplock plastic bag!

LAYER THE APPLIQUÉS

1. Working on a heat-resistant surface (ironing board, large folded bath towel, etc.), position a Teflon appliqué pressing sheet or baker's parchment paper on the pressing surface.

2. To make a placement guide for each appliqué element, trace the appliqué patterns on a piece of transparent plastic such as vinyl, Mylar, a clear page protector, or a plastic bag. Pin this master pattern to the pressing surface along one edge over the pressing area.

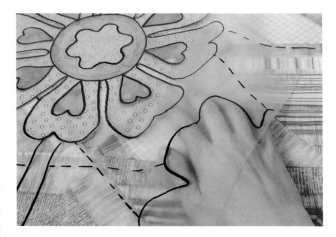

3. Peel away the paper backing from each pattern piece.

4. Position the largest appliqué base pieces first. Layer each component over the previous one, building the design shape. Refer to the photograph (page 61) or transparent guide for the placement of all the design elements.

5. Once all the pieces are in the correct position, iron the layers together. (Do not fuse to the quilt top yet.) If you are using the placement guide, flip it out of the way before pressing.

EMBELLISH THE APPLIQUÉS

1. Attach a cording foot or an open-toe appliqué foot to your sewing machine, and prepare it for machine appliqué.

2. Cut pieces of tear-away stabilizer, and place a piece beneath each of the larger appliqué motifs. Machine appliqué the smaller appliqué shapes to the larger appliqué shape (e.g., hearts onto flower petals, small flower centers over large flower centers) beneath it using one of the following methods:

Outline the shapes with either matching or contrasting thread and a decorative stitch or satin stitch. Vary the line and stitch pattern thickness for more interest.

Stitch with a zigzag stitch over black or color-coordinated craft cord (known as couching) for a solid continuous outline around each shape.

Note: Do *not* stitch the outer edges of the appliqué shape in this step.

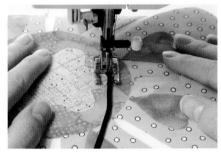

Appliqué with cording and open-toe foot

3. Carefully remove the tear-away stabilizer from behind the appliqué shapes.

APPLIQUÉ THE DESIGNS

1. Position the leaf, stem, flower, dragonfly, and hummingbird appliqué shapes on the quilt top, referring to the photograph on page 61 and the quilt diagram at right for placement guidance if you wish.

2. Fuse the shapes to the quilt top.

3. Pin or spray (with temporary fabric adhesive) a new piece of tear-away stabilizer to the wrong side of the quilt top behind the appliqué shapes, or use a single piece of stabilizer behind each shape.

4. Stitch around each shape using one of the options as given in Step 2 under Embellish the Appliqué.

5. Pin the black-and-white strip to the quilt top to create the impression of a flight path behind the dragonfly. Refer to the photograph on page 61 for placement guidance. Press with steam to flatten the strip and hold the curves. Hand appliqué or topstitch by machine on both sides of the strip. Place stabilizer underneath if stitching by machine.

6. Remove all remaining stabilizer from the wrong side of the quilt top. Press from the wrong side.

Finishing

Layer the quilt top with the batting and backing, and baste. Quilt as desired, and bind.

Quilt diagram

- Quick Chevron Diamond
- fast2cut Fussy Cutter diamond ruler 3″ or fast2cut half-diamond ruler 6½″; or 3″ diamond template pattern (pullout page P2)

Skill level: Advanced beginner

Finished Block size: 2⅜″ diamond

FIRE STORM

58″ × 38¼″, 2008, by Jan Krentz; machine quilting by Janet Sturdevant Stuart, Fort Worth, TX

The vibrant colors of the printed stripe I used in this quilt remind me of the wildfires that ravage drought-stricken land. My town and many others have suffered loss of life and property during wildfires in recent years.

Any interesting printed stripe will be transformed into a stylized landscape with this simple technique!

Fabric Requirements and Cutting

Refer to Prewashing Guidelines on page 9 to determine whether to wash your fabrics before cutting and sewing. See Cutting Half Diamonds, beginning on page 15, for details on cutting stripes and mirror-image designs as needed. Layer the fabric wrong sides together, aligning the stripes. Cut 3″ strips aligned with the stripe pattern through 2 layers.

YARDAGE	FOR	CUTTING
2½ yards bright-colored, large-scale striped fabric	Half diamonds	Cut approximately 221 diamonds, 3″. Cut in half widthwise to yield 442 half diamonds.
1⅞ yards dark fabric	Borders	Cut on the lengthwise grain: 2 strips, 1″ × 62″ 2 strips, 1″ × 42″ 2 strips, 3½″ × 62″ 2 strips, 3½″ × 42″
¼ yard contrasting fabric	Narrow accent trim	Cut 6 strips, 1″ × 42″.
⅝ yard fabric	Binding	Cut 6 strips, 2¾″ × 42″.
3 yards fabric	Backing	

Batting: 66″ × 46″

Quilt Assembly

Be sure to read Construction Techniques, beginning on page 23, before beginning your project.

1. Working on the design wall, match pairs of half diamonds according to the printed stripe to create a chevron pattern. Create an overall composition, grouping the colors together, moving from one color family to the next, and placing the half diamonds in 17 vertical rows of 26 half diamonds each.

2. When you are satisfied with the composition, construct the quilt top by either sewing vertical rows or sewing diamonds and then sewing them together in diagonal rows. Press and trim to square or straighten the quilt top's edges.

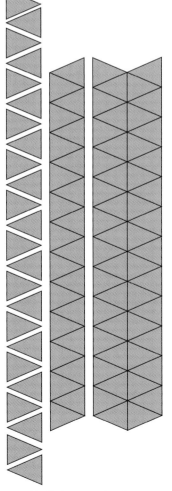

Vertical row construction

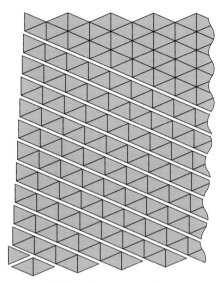

Diagonal row construction

3. Piece together the 1″ accent strips, and cut them into 2 strips 62″ long and 2 strips 42″ long. Sew a 1″ narrow trim strip to the edge of each 3½″ border by following the instructions in Adding Narrow Accent Trim to Mitered Borders, page 37. Press and grade the seam allowance of the trim strip.

4. Sew a 1″ inner border to each wider border to create 4 border units. Press.

5. Add the borders to the quilt top, following the directions in Mitered Borders, page 34.

6. Layer the quilt top with the batting and backing, and baste. Quilt as desired. Bind.

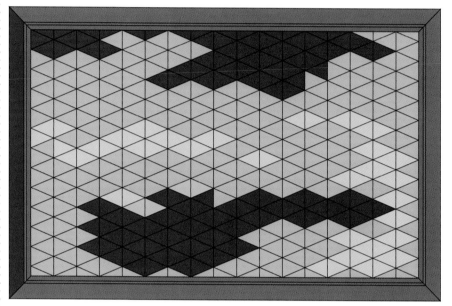

Quilt diagram

- Framed Diamond

- fast2cut Fussy Cutter 45° diamond ruler 6½″,
half-diamond ruler 6½″, and quarter-diamond ruler 6½″;
or 6½″ diamond template pattern, 6½″ half-diamond template
pattern, and 6½″ quarter-diamond template pattern (pullout page P2)

Skill level: Intermediate

Finished Block size: 6″ diamond

DANCING AFRICAN LADIES

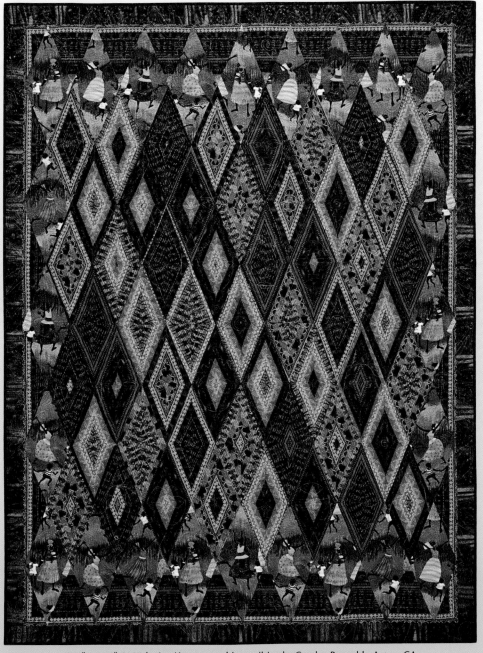

63½″ × 82½″, 2007, by Jan Krentz; machine quilting by Carolyn Reynolds, Acton, CA

Create a striking quilt from two or three coordinating fabrics—a focal print, a stripe, and a border fabric. The attractive Framed Diamonds in the center of the quilt were cut from various areas within the same printed stripe, creating an overall mosaic pattern reminiscent of woven yarn God's Eyes or tile work. You can incorporate the theme print within the center diamonds, if desired, for more variety.

Fabric Requirements and Cutting

Refer to Prewashing Guidelines on page 9 to determine whether to wash your fabrics before cutting and sewing. See Cutting Techniques, beginning on page 11, and Fussy Cutting Motifs on page 13 for details on cutting methods as needed. Cut the strips for the Framed Diamonds following the directions in Strip-Piecing Framed Diamonds, page 31; determine which areas of the striped fabric are your favorite, and cut as many of those as possible. Note that this cutting technique requires extra fabric and will result in leftover pieces. Use the extra fabric in another project, or sew pieces together to use for the quilt backing.

To achieve the effect of a striped inner border in the pieced center of the quilt, fussy cut the half diamonds, long half diamonds (split diamonds lengthwise), and corner pieces as directed in the cutting chart.

YARDAGE	FOR	CUTTING
2 to 3 yards theme fabric* (African ladies or other large-scale print with motifs that are no more than 4" to 4½" tall and 4" wide)	Fussy-cut diamonds	Fussy cut 24 diamonds, 6½".
5 to 6 yards companion stripe	Framed Diamonds	Cut 4½" diagonal mirror-image strips at a 22.5° angle.
	Inner top and bottom borders	Cut 16 half diamonds, 6½".**
	Inner side borders	Cut 8 split diamonds, 6½".†
	Inner border corners	Cut 4 rectangles, 4" × 9½", and 4 rectangles, 4" × 5".††
2½ yards fabric (1 yard if cut crosswise and pieced)	Outer border	Cut 2 strips, 3" × 68", lengthwise. Cut 2 strips, 3" × 87", lengthwise.
¾ yard fabric	Binding	Cut 8 strips, 2¾" × 42".
5¾ yards fabric	Backing and hanging sleeve	
Batting: 72" × 91"		

*Yardage varies depending on the size of the motifs and the number of repeats in the design.

**Align the bottom (short) edge of the half-diamond ruler with the same stripe in each.

†Fold a 17" section of fabric in half with the fold perpendicular to the stripes. Place the quarter-diamond template on the folded fabric, aligning the dashed ¼" seamline on the short edge of the ruler with the fold of the fabric and the long straight edge of the ruler with the same stripe you chose for the half diamonds. Each cut will produce 1 long half diamond.

††Align one long side with the same stripe you chose for the inner border half diamonds and split diamonds.

Quilt Assembly

Be sure to read Construction Techniques, beginning on page 23, before beginning your project.

1. Make 53 Framed Diamonds by following the instructions in Cutting Angled Strips for Framed Diamonds, page 20.

jan's tip

Cut and piece small quantities of diamonds systematically to avoid cutting too many undesirable pieces. Optional: Substitute fussy-cut theme-fabric diamonds for some of the Framed Diamonds for variety.

2. Arrange the Framed Diamonds on the design wall in rows. Place the fussy-cut diamonds around the sides, top, and bottom.

3. Add long half diamonds along the sides and half diamonds along the top and bottom.

4. You will need to piece the inner border corners so that the stripe will appear to turn the corner at a right angle. Place a 4″ × 5″ rectangle on top of the right end of a 9½″ × 4″ rectangle, right sides together, aligning the printed stripes. Place the second 4″ × 5″ rectangle on the left end of a 9½″ × 4″ rectangle. Make 2 of each.

5. Draw a line at a 45° angle ⅜″ from the lower corner of the fabrics. Sew on the pencil line. Open to check the match of the stripes and check that the corner is square. When you are satisfied, trim the extra fabric ¼″ beyond the stitching, and press the seam open.

Match the prints on the corner border pieces, and mark a diagonal sewing line. Sew on the drawn line.

6. Position the quarter-diamond ruler on the corner, and cut along the angled edge to trim away excess fabric.

Trim to create 4 inner border corners.

7. Construct the quilt top by sewing diagonal rows of diamonds, with a split-diamond unit at each end. See Sewing Diagonal Rows of Diamonds, page 25. Add the corner pieces last.

Quilt diagram

8. Add the outer border with straight or mitered corners, as you prefer. See Borders, page 32.

9. Layer the quilt top with the batting and backing, and baste. Quilt as desired. Bind.

■ 6″ × 12″ ruler or 4″ × 8″ ruler

Skill level: Skilled beginner and above

Finished Block size: 5½″ × 11½″ or 3½″ × 7½″

MOSAIC TILES

60″ × 49″, 2008, by Jan Krentz; machine quilting by Janet Sturdevant Stuart, Fort Worth, TX

The Faux Diamond quilt is one of my favorite designs because it is so easy to cut and sew! Select any fun printed-stripe fabric and embellish with a whimsical rickrack border.

I used an odd-size rectangle to make my Mosaic Tiles quilt. I've written these instructions with simplified cutting so that you can use either a 6″ × 12″ or 4″ × 8″ ruler to cut the blocks.

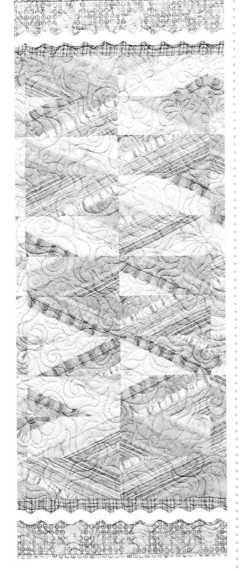

Fabric Requirements and Cutting

Refer to Prewashing Guidelines on page 9 to determine whether to wash your fabrics before cutting and sewing. See Cutting Rectangles for Faux Diamonds on page 22 for details on cutting as needed.

MOSAIC TILES, LARGE VERSION

Quilt size: 83″ × 74½″   Ruler: 6″ × 12″

YARDAGE	FOR	CUTTING
4–6 yards printed stripe	Blocks	Cut 66 rectangles, 6″ × 12″ (33 angled right, 33 angled left).
⅝ yard print fabric	Border 1	Cut 8 strips, 2″ × 42″.
2½ yards print fabric	Border 2	Cut 2 strips, 6″ × 79″, lengthwise. Cut 2 strips, 6″ × 87″, lengthwise.
⅞ yard fabric	Binding	Cut 9 strips, 2¾″ × 42″.
8½ yards jumbo rickrack	Border trim (optional)	
7¼ yards fabric	Backing	

Batting: 91″ × 83″

MOSAIC TILES, SMALLER VERSION

Quilt size: 55″ × 48½″   Ruler: 4″ × 8″

YARDAGE	FOR	CUTTING
2–4 yards printed stripe	Blocks	Cut 66 rectangles, 4″ × 8″ (33 angled right, 33 angled left).
⅜ yard print fabric	Border 1	Cut 5 strips, 2″ × 42″.
1¾ yards print fabric	Border 2	Cut 2 strips, 4″ × 52″, lengthwise. Cut 2 strips, 4″ × 60″, lengthwise.
⅝ yard fabric	Binding	Cut 6 strips, 2¾″ × 42″.
5½ yards jumbo rickrack	Border trim (optional)	
3½ yards fabric	Backing	

Batting: 63″ × 57″

Quilt Assembly

Be sure to read Construction Techniques, beginning on page 23, before beginning your project. For best results, starch the fabric before cutting.

1. Arrange the rectangles on the design wall in 11 horizontal rows of 6 rectangles each; move the pieces around until you are pleased with your design.

2. Sew the rectangles into rows. Press.

3. Sew the rows together. Press.

4. Sew the 2″ border strips together end to end to create 1 long strip. Cut the strip into 2 lengths, 68″, and 2 lengths, 76″, for the larger quilt (46″ and 52″ for the smaller quilt).

5. Assemble the border strips and sew them onto the quilt, following the instructions in Mitered Borders, page 34. Press.

Optional: Pin jumbo rickrack over the seam between borders 1 and 2. Fold the corners neatly. Topstitch the rickrack to the quilt top.

6. Layer the quilt top with the batting and backing, and baste. Quilt as desired. Bind.

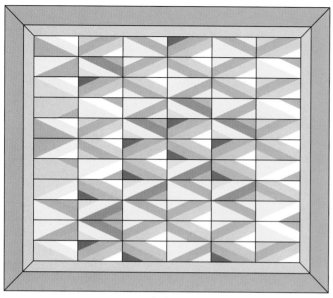

Quilt diagram

OTHER BORDER AND EMBELLISHMENT OPTIONS

- Add appliquéd leaves, vines, or flowers.

- Add lace between borders 1 and 2.

- Appliqué cut-out motifs from a coordinating fabric.

- Appliqué photo-transfer images.

- Appliqué lettering such as "Happy Birthday," "Spring," "Summer," "Fall," "Winter," "Welcome," and so on.

- Embellish with bows, ribbon, charms, buttons, or other items.

- Sew small circles or squares of fuzzy hook-and-loop tape (Velcro) to the quilt top. Attach the "hook" side to plastic toys, calendar numbers (to create a nativity calendar), children's school photos (for a school teacher's class roster), or other fun dimensional objects.

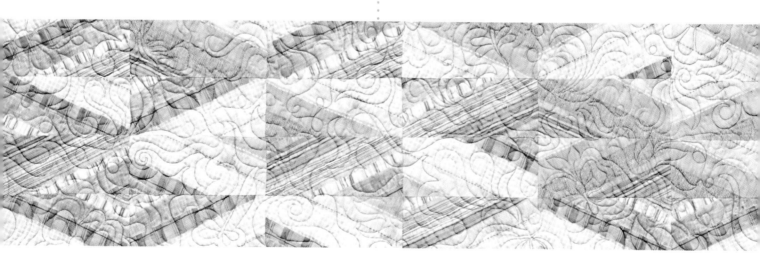

■ 6″ × 12″ ruler or 4″ × 8″ ruler

Skill level: Skilled beginner and above

Finished Block size: 5½″ × 11½″ or 3½″ × 7½″

MARDI GRAS

19″ × 46″ table runner, 2008, by Jan Krentz

Try the Faux Diamond technique to create a fast, fun table runner from one colorful printed stripe. Add contrasting narrow borders and it's complete! Use either size option to create your own variation.

Fabric Requirements and Cutting

Refer to Prewashing Guidelines on page 9 to determine whether to wash your fabrics before cutting and sewing. See Cutting Rectangles for Faux Diamonds on page 22 for details on the cutting method as needed.

MARDI GRAS, LARGE VERSION

Table runner size: 26″ × 52″   Ruler: 6″ × 12″

YARDAGE	FOR	CUTTING
2 to 2½ yards multicolored stripe*	Blocks	Cut 16 rectangles, 6″ × 12″ (8 angled right, 8 angled left).
⅜ yard narrow black-and-white stripe	Border 1, long sides	Cut 3 strips, 1″ × 42″.
	Border 1, short sides	Cut 2 strips, 2″ × 23½″.
⅜ yard gold fabric	Border 2, long sides	Cut 3 strips, 2″ × 42″.
	Border 2, short sides	Cut 2 strips, 2″ × 26½″.
½ yard fabric	Binding	Cut 5 strips, 2¾″ × 42″.
1¾ yards fabric	Backing	
Batting: 32″ × 58″		

Yardage varies depending on the stripe width.

MARDI GRAS, SMALLER VERSION

Table runner size: 18″ × 36″   Ruler: 4″ × 8″

YARDAGE	FOR	CUTTING
1 to 1½ yards multicolored stripe fabric*	Blocks	Cut 16 rectangles, 4″ × 8″ (8 angled right, 8 angled left).
¼ yard narrow black-and-white stripe	Border 1, long sides	Cut 2 strips, 1″ × 30½″.
	Border 1, short sides	Cut 2 strips, 2″ × 15½″.
¼ yard gold fabric	Border 2, long sides	Cut 2 strips, 2″ × 33½″.
	Border 2, short sides	Cut 2 strips, 2″ × 18½″.
⅜ yard fabric	Binding	Cut 3 strips, 2¾″ × 42″.
1⅛ yards fabric	Backing	
Batting: 22″ × 40″		

Yardage varies depending on the stripe width.

Quilt Assembly

Be sure to read Construction Techniques, beginning on page 23, before beginning your project.

1. Arrange the rectangles on the design wall in 4 rows of 4 rectangles each. Move the pieces around until you are pleased with your design.

2. Sew the rectangles into rows. Press.

3. Sew the rows together. Press.

4. You will need to piece the borders for the larger table runner. Sew the 3 black-and-white 1″ × 42″ strips together end to end; cut into 2 strips, 1″ × 46½″. Sew the 3 gold 2″ × 42″ strips together end to end; cut into 2 strips, 2″ × 49½″.

5. Sew borders 1 and 2 to the quilt, adding the side borders first. See Borders with Butted Corners, page 33, for more details.

6. Layer the quilt top with the batting and backing, and baste. Quilt as desired. Bind.

Quilt diagram

- Quarter-diamond method: fast2cut Fussy Cutter quarter-diamond ruler 6½″, and half-diamond ruler 6½″; or 6½″ quarter-diamond template pattern and 6½″ half-diamond template pattern (pullout page P2)

- Faux Diamond method: 6″ × 12″ ruler

Skill level: Intermediate and above

Finished Block size: 6″ diamond or 3¼″ × 7¾″ rectangle

STONE MOSAIC

58″ × 37″, 2008, by Jan Krentz; machine quilting by Janet Sturdevant Stuart, Fort Worth, TX

This dynamite quilt was inspired by European stone mosaic floors. The subtle shading of black, white, and three shades of gray is combined with warm earthy colors. The design would be equally intriguing in cool tones of blues and greens or hot fiery red, orange, and fuchsia pink. Display your mosaic design either horizontally or vertically.

You can cut this design with the quarter-diamond ruler, or you can use the rectangular Faux Diamond technique from strip-pieced fabrics. The quarter-diamond method takes less fabric, but the Faux Diamond method is easier to piece.

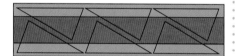

Quarter-diamond units are cut from strip sets.

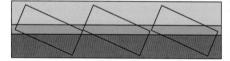

Rectangles are cut from the strip sets for the Faux Diamond technique.

Fabric Requirements and Cutting

Refer to Prewashing Guidelines on page 9 to determine whether to wash your fabrics before cutting and sewing. See Cutting Techniques, beginning on page 11, for details on cutting methods as needed.

If you are short on fabric, I recommend using the quarter-diamond ruler method. If you have adequate yardage, piecing with the Faux Diamond method is easier, but results in slightly more waste between cut shapes. Purchase the larger

amount of fabric for the Faux Diamond method. Use starch and iron fabrics before cutting with either method to provide stability when cutting and piecing.

The quilt size may be adjusted easily by cutting fewer or more units than specified. You will typically be able to cut 4 units from each full-width strip set. Note that the 4″ strips are cut slightly wider than needed for easy and accurate custom cutting.

YARDAGE	FOR	CUTTING	
		Quarter Diamond	**Faux Diamond**
			Cut 1 strip, 4″ × 11″.
½ to ⅝ yard light gray	Diamond strips	Cut 6 strips, 2″ × 42″.	Cut 6 strips, 2″ × 42″. Cut 1 strip, 2″ × 11″.
⅝ to ⅞ yard medium gray	Diamond strips	Cut 4 strips, 4″ × 42″.	Cut 5 strips, 4″ × 42″.
½ to 1 yard dark charcoal gray	Diamond strips	Cut 3 strips, 4″ × 42″.	Cut 6 strips, 4″ × 42″.
½ to ¾ yard black	Diamond strips	Cut 3 strips, 4″ × 42″.	Cut 4 strips, 4″ × 42″. Cut 1 strip, 4″ × 11″.
1½ to 1¾ yards gold	Quarter diamonds, half diamonds, or diamond strips	Cut 8 half diamonds, 6½″, and 4 quarter diamonds, 6½″. Cut 2 strips, 2″ × 42″.	Cut 6 strips, 4″ × 42″. Subcut 2 strips into 1 strip, 4″ × 22″, and 3 strips, 4″ × 11″. Cut 1 strip, 2″ × 42″.
	Outer border	Cut 3 strips, 3½″ × 42″. Sew end to end to create long borders.	Cut 3 strips, 3½″ × 42″. Sew end to end to create long borders.
	Binding	Cut 2¾″ strips to total 104″ (straight grain or bias).	Cut 2¾″ strips to total 104″ (straight grain or bias).
1½ to 1¾ yard olive green	Quarter diamonds, half diamonds, or diamond strips	Cut 8 half diamonds, 6½″, and 4 quarter diamonds, 6½″. Cut 1 strip, 2″ × 42″.	Cut 6 strips, 4″ × 42″. Subcut 2 strips into 1 strip, 4″ × 22″, and 3 strips, 4″ × 11″. Cut 1 strip, 2″ × 42″.
	Outer border	Cut 3 strips, 3½″ × 42″. Sew end to end to create long borders.	Cut 3 strips, 3½″ × 42″. Sew end to end to create long borders.
	Binding	Cut 2¾″ strips to total 104″ (straight grain or bias).	Cut 2¾″ strips to total 104″ (straight grain or bias).
¼ yard each of 2 different greens	Diamond strips	Cut 6 strips, 2″ × 42″.	Cut 6 strips, 2″ × 42″.
½ yard total of medium-value yellow-orange, orange, and red-orange fabrics	Diamond strips	Cut 6 strips, 2″ × 42″.	Cut 5 strips, 2″ × 42″.
½ yard total of 3 to 6 brown fabrics	Diamond strips	Cut 6 strips, 2″ × 42″.	Cut 6 strips, 2″ × 42″. Cut 1 strip, 2″ × 11″.
2¾ yards fabric	Backing		

Batting: 66″ × 45″

Quilt Assembly

Be sure to read Construction Techniques, beginning on page 23, before beginning your project.

The four values—white, medium gray, charcoal gray, and black—remain constant in the center of each diamond block. The longer sections create the outer frames of the diamonds. The sides of the diamonds vary in color. The light gray fabric is in the same position in each block—in the upper left. A green is in the upper right; a brown is in the lower right; and a gold, orange, or red-orange is in the lower left position.

QUARTER-DIAMOND METHOD

To use the quarter-diamond ruler, combine 4″ and 2″ strips to make strip sets. Each strip set will yield 8 quarter-diamond units.

1. Sew a white 4″ strip between 2 light gray 2″ strips. Make 3 strip sets, and press the seams toward the light gray. Cut 22 quarter diamonds with the ruler wrong side up.

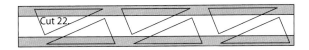

2. Sew a medium gray 4″ strip between 2 orange or red-orange 2″ strips. Make 3 strip sets, and press the seams toward the medium gray. Cut 17 quarter diamonds with the ruler right side up.

3. Sew a medium gray 4″ strip between 2 gold 2″ strips. Make 1 strip set, and press the seams toward the medium gray. Cut 5 quarter diamonds with the ruler right side up.

4. Sew a dark charcoal gray 4″ strip between 2 green 2″ strips. Make 3 strip sets, and press the seams toward the dark gray. Cut 22 quarter diamonds with the ruler right side up.

5. Sew a black 4″ strip between 2 brown 2″ strips. Make 3 strip sets, and press the seams toward the brown. Cut 22 quarter diamonds with the ruler wrong side up.

6. Sew the quarter diamonds together to create the 22 complete diamonds. Be sure to keep the position of the colors and values consistent in each diamond.

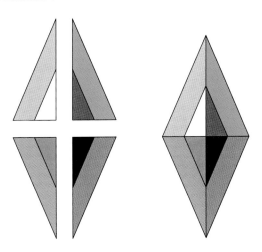

7. Arrange the pieced diamonds, half diamonds, and quarter diamonds on the design wall, keeping the colors in the same positions as shown in the assembly diagram below. Vary the placement of orange, red orange, and gold as in the photo or as desired.

8. Sew the quilt top together in diagonal rows. See Sewing Diagonal Rows of Diamonds, page 25.

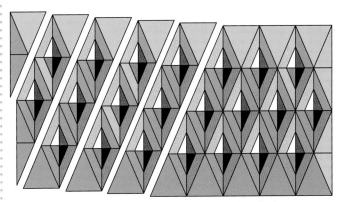

Quilt assembly diagram, quarter-diamond method

FAUX DIAMOND METHOD

To use the Faux Diamond method, you will sew the 2″ and 4″ strips to make a series of strip sets.

Note: When cutting Faux Diamond rectangles, it's very important that you place the corner of the finished rectangle at the quarter-inch seam allowance on the diagonal line, rather than the corners of the rectangle ruler.

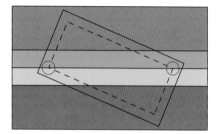

Align the seam allowance corners with the seam (circled), not the ruler corners.

1. Prepare a 6″ × 12″ ruler for cutting the odd-size rectangles. Mark the ruler with narrow strips of blue tape (see page 17) to highlight the 3¾″ × 8¼″ area to cut. Then use a Sharpie marker to make dots at the corners where the ¼″ seam allowances intersect. Place the dots on the appropriate seams when cutting.

2. Make strip sets from the 42″ strips as shown. Press the seams to the side in opposite directions for the units angled to the right and those angled to the left. You can press all the seams open if you prefer. Cut 3¾″ × 8¼″ rectangles as shown. Cut 2 adjacent sides first, then pick up the ruler and rotate it, aligning the tape on the ruler with the newly cut edges, and cut the 2 remaining sides.

Rotate your cutting mat as needed so that you are not cutting toward yourself or in an unsafe manner. Pay close attention to the angle of the rectangles in the diagrams.

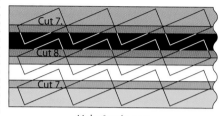

Make 2 strip sets.

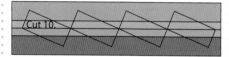

Make 2 strip sets.

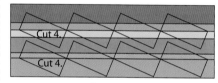

Make 1 strip set.

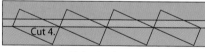

Make 3 strip sets.

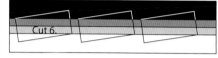

Make 1 strip set.

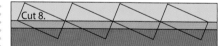

Make 2 strip sets.

3. Make strip sets from the shorter strips as shown. Cut rectangles from each combination.

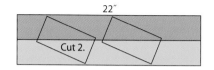

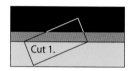

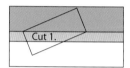

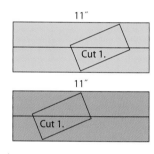

Make 1 strip set each.

4. You should have a total of 64 rectangles as shown. Note the angle of the seams; 32 units are angled right, and 32 units are angled left.

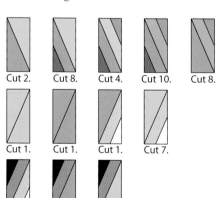

Cut 2.	Cut 8.	Cut 4.	Cut 10.	Cut 8.
Cut 1.	Cut 1.	Cut 1.	Cut 7.	
Cut 14.	Cut 7.	Cut 1.		

5. Arrange the pieced rectangles on the design wall according to the assembly diagram shown below. Sew together in rows; then sew the rows together.

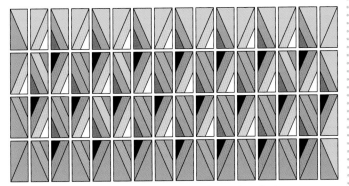

Quilt assembly diagram, Faux Diamond method

BORDERS

For this quilt you will need to create mitered borders that match the angles of the diamonds.

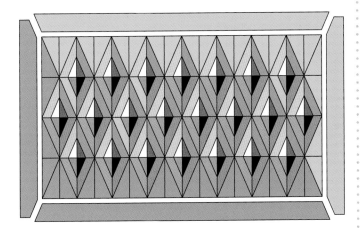

1. Sew the 3 gold border strips end to end, creating 1 long strip. Cut into 1 piece 66" long and 1 piece 45" long. Repeat for the 3 green border strips.

2. Straighten the quilt top by trimming slightly if necessary, and measure to verify that both opposite edges are the same length.

3. Mark each corner of the quilt top with a dot ¼" from both edges on the seam line, and measure the length of each side from dot to dot.

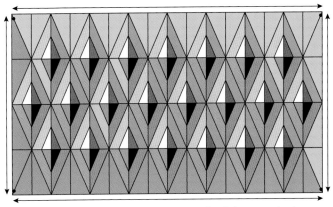

Mark a dot at each corner, and measure each side between the dots .

4. Mark the lengths from Step 3 on each border strip, centering the distance. Place dots where the seams will intersect at the corners. Using a quilter's ruler with a square corner, mark a faint line 90° from the seam ends (dots) on each border end.

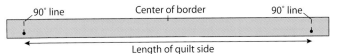

Length of quilt side

5. Begin with the side borders. Place the quarter-diamond ruler with the short edge parallel to the 90° line on the right end of the border; align the hole in the ruler over the dot on the border. Lightly draw along the edge. Repeat for the left border end, turning the ruler upside down. Repeat for the second side border. Note: The angle should mimic and extend the angle from the adjacent quilt block.

6. Cut on the marked line.

Side borders. Make 1 green and 1 gold.

7. Mark the top and bottom borders in the same manner, but place the ruler so that the long side is parallel to the 90° line.

Top and bottom borders. Make 1 green and 1 gold.

8. Sew the borders to the quilt top stitching from dot to dot. See Mitered Borders, page 34, for stitching tips. Note that for this quilt, the angle is different and the fabric has already been trimmed for the diagonal seam allowance. Trim and square up the corners after stitching.

9. Layer the quilt top with the batting and backing, and baste. Quilt as desired.

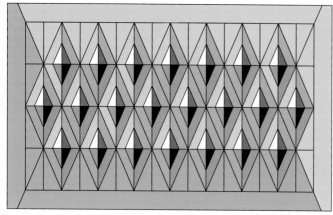

Quilt diagram

BINDING

You will need to join the gold and green binding strips at the same angle as the border where they meet near the corners of the quilt. Use the quarter-diamond ruler for this.

1. Join the 3 gold binding strips end to end using the standard diagonal seam to create 1 long strip. Repeat with the 3 green binding strips.

2. Place the green binding strip along the green edges of the quilt, pinning to position the color split exactly at the seam. Pin carefully at the corners near the 2-color join. Repeat with the gold binding strip.

3. Beginning a few inches below the pinned green/gold corner, sew the green binding to the side and bottom edges, creating a folded miter at the green corner. Stop sewing about 8″ from where the gold binding begins.

4. Repeat Step 3 with the gold binding, beginning about 8″ from the green/gold join along the top of the quilt and stopping a few inches from the bottom corner.

5. Remove the quilt from the machine. Position the binding ends in place up to the exact line where the colors should change. Mark the area to be joined with a pin, angling it in the direction you want the seam to run. Mark a line on the wrong side of the binding, using the quarter-diamond ruler, and add ¼″ for seam allowances. Repeat for the other binding tail. You may have to remove the pins around the corner to do this. Pin, and sew the seam with basting stitches.

6. Audition the stitched binding against the quilt top. Does it fit perfectly? Does the seam run the same direction as the quilt's colored blocks? Once you are satisfied, sew the binding with a shorter stitch length. Trim the seam allowance, and press the seam open. Apply the remainder of the binding to the quilt top.

7. Repeat Steps 5 and 6 for the other binding ends.

8. Turn the binding to the back, and stitch by hand.

- fast2cut Fussy Cutter 45° diamond rulers 6½″ and 3″; or 6½″ diamond template pattern and 3″ diamond template pattern (pullout page P2)

Skill level: Skilled beginner

AURORA

72″ × 42″, 2008, by Jan Krentz; machine quilting by D'Andrea Mitchell, San Diego, CA

This gorgeous art quilt was created with simple techniques. Three different colorations of the same printed fabric were used to create the glowing panels and floating diamonds. The design is suitable for batiks, hand-dyed yardage, or gradation prints that change color from selvage to selvage.

The Aurora quilt features five narrow panels, but you can modify the design with any number of narrow panels and surface diamonds. Simple panels are cut and arranged across the background. Various-sized 45° diamonds are cut from different areas on the remainder of the fabric to create variable-colored diamonds.

Fabric Requirements and Cutting

Refer to Prewashing Guidelines on page 9 to determine whether to wash your fabrics before cutting and sewing. See Cutting Techniques, beginning on page 11, for details on cutting methods as needed.

YARDAGE	FOR	CUTTING
2¼ yards gradient fabric 1	Background	Make a straightening cut along the 2 raw edges.
1½ to 2 yards gradient fabric 2	Background panels	Cut 2 panels, 11″ × 36″.
		Cut 1 panel, 13″ × 35″.
	Diamonds	Cut 20 to 25 diamonds in assorted sizes.*
1½ to 2 yards gradient fabric 3	Background panels	Cut 2 panels, 9″ × 34″.
	Diamonds	Cut 25 to 30 diamonds in assorted sizes.*
3¼ yards fabric	Backing	
⅝ yard fabric	Binding	Cut 6 strips, 2¾″ × 42″.
Batting: 80″ × 50″		
6 to 8 yards 18″-wide tear-away stabilizer		
¼″-wide fusible web (40-yard roll)		
Brown craft paper or appliqué pressing sheet		
Freezer paper		
Heat-resistant design wall or beach towels layered on a large table		

*See instructions in Step 7, page 85.

Quilt Assembly

Be sure to read Construction Techniques, beginning on page 23, before beginning your project.

1. Zigzag or serge the raw edges of the 2-yard background panel. Leave the selvage edges on for now.

2. Secure the background to a heat-resistant surface or design wall, or lay the fabric on multiple beach towels over a large table.

3. Cover your ironing board with brown paper, freezer paper (shiny side down), or an appliqué pressing sheet.

4. Position a panel wrong side up on the ironing surface. Cut ¼″-wide fusible web strips to match the lengths of the panels. Working with 1 adhesive strip at a time, place the pebbly rough surface (adhesive side) toward the fabric, aligning the adhesive at the outer edge of the panel. Press adhesive strips with a hot iron, following the manufacturer's instructions, to create a continuous row of fusible web strips along all the edges. Repeat for all 5 panels. Remove the paper backing.

5. Position each narrow panel on the background as shown in the quilt diagram below. Arrange the fabrics to maximize the color contrast against the background fabric. Measure the distance from each panel to the edges of the background to position them evenly. Use the dimensions in the diagram as a guide, or place the panels as you like. The arrangement may vary depending upon your fabric and the width.

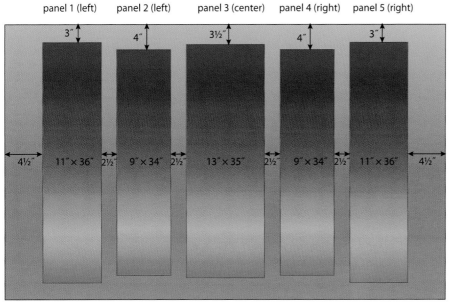

panel 1 (left) panel 2 (left) panel 3 (center) panel 4 (right) panel 5 (right)

3″ 4″ 3½″ 4″ 3″

4½″ 11″ × 36″ 2½″ 9″ × 34″ 2½″ 13″ × 35″ 2½″ 9″ × 34″ 2½″ 11″ × 36″ 4½″

Quilt diagram

6. Using an iron on the design wall or heat-resistant surface, press the panels at the edges, securing them to the background fabric. Pin the panels in place first if you must move the fabric to an ironing board or pressing surface.

7. Align the diamond ruler over dyed or printed streaks on the fabric. If the fabric is streaked in a linear pattern, align the ruler so the pattern fills the diamond from tip to tip lengthwise. Cut various-sized diamonds (from 1″ to 8″) from fabrics 2 and 3, using both the large and small diamond rulers.

To cut 7″ diamonds: Cut a freezer-paper strip 7″ wide × 17″ long (or other width and length). Trim the opposing ends off at a 45° angle (cutting parallel lines), creating an oversized diamond template. Press the shiny side down over either fabric 2 or 3—the template will cling to the fabric. Cover the template with an acrylic ruler or diamond ruler, and cut along the edges to cut out the oversized diamond.

jan's tip

Remember, when creating your own templates, the diamond shape should measure the same from parallel edge to parallel edge in both directions. To make a freezer-paper template of any size, draw parallel lines the desired diamond size. Connect them by drawing a 45° line at one end. Then measure over the same distance as between the parallel lines to draw the second parallel 45° line.

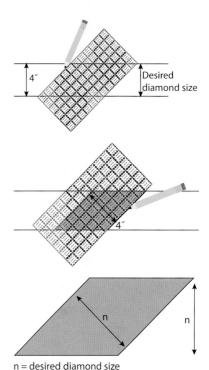

4″ Desired diamond size

4″

n n

n = desired diamond size

8. Place the assorted diamonds wrong side up on the protected ironing board. Cut and press ¼" fusible web strips to the outer edges of all the diamond shapes. Remove the paper backing.

9. Arrange the diamonds in an asymmetrical arrangement on the panels. Position single diamonds, pairs, or clusters of 3 or 4 diamonds on the panel background, referring to the placement guide below and photo (page 83). Maintain the vertical alignment of all the diamonds as you position them in an attractive arrangement. Overlap diamonds on the panel edge here and there to create a floating effect.

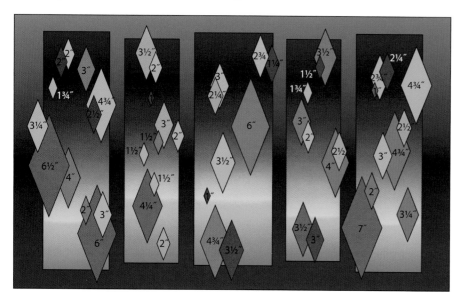

10. Pin a piece of tear-away stabilizer behind 1 panel.

11. Select coordinating variegated threads, and machine appliqué the edges of each panel and each diamond. Take several small "lock stitches" at the beginning and end of each appliqué stitching sequence to secure the threads. Change thread colors as you prefer, or use the same color of variegated thread for all the diamonds and panels.

12. After all the motifs and panels have been stitched to the background, turn the piece wrong side up on the table. Carefully tear away or trim the stabilizer from the back of the piece, leaving a small amount beneath the stitches.

13. Layer the quilt top with the batting and backing, and baste. Quilt as desired. Bind.

Optional Embellishments and Variations

Embellish the quilt with couching (before layering and quilting), textile paints, beading, crystals, netting, foils, or other items to further personalize it.

Create single, double, or triple panels plus appliquéd diamonds on any size background. Cut a narrow background to make table runners and narrow wallhangings. A grouping of 3 narrow wallhangings would make an effective and dramatic display up a stairwell or in an office setting.

■ fast2cut half-diamond ruler 6½"; or 6½" half-diamond
template pattern (pullout page P1)

Skill level: Intermediate

SUPER SCOOPS

42" × 49½", 2008, by Jan Krentz; machine quilting by Janet Stuart, Fort Worth, TX

"You scream, I scream, We ALL scream for ice cream!" This fun saying inspired my whimsical wall quilt. I cut several rusty-colored fabric "sugar cones" using the half-diamond ruler and used a collection of marbled and textured fabrics that resemble delicious ice cream flavors and treats. I topped off the delicacies with fun embellishment "sprinkles." Bon appétit!

Fabric Requirements and Cutting

Refer to Prewashing Guidelines on page 9 to determine whether to wash your fabrics before cutting and sewing. Follow the steps in Ice Cream Cones and Scoops on page 90 when cutting the appliqué shapes. See pullout page 1 for the applique patterns.

YARDAGE	FOR	CUTTING
1 to 1¼ yards light-colored fabric*	Background	Cut 1 rectangle, 34½" × 42". (Remove selvages.)
½ yard lavender fabric	Accent panel	Cut 1 rectangle, 18" × 36".
½ yard green fabric	Accent panel	Cut 1 rectangle, 15" × 30".
⅓ yard blue fabric	Accent panel	Cut 1 rectangle, 10" × 20".
¼ yard black with white polka dot	Narrow accent trim	Cut 4 strips, 1" × 42".
1½ yards printed stripe	Border	Cut 5 strips, 4½" × 42".
5 pieces, 8" × 10" each, of copper, rust, or brown fabrics	Waffle cones	Cut 1 half diamond, 6½", from each fabric.
10 to 12 different fat eighths (9" × 20") of pastel fabrics (marbled textures)	Ice cream	Cut appliqué shapes from template patterns.
1 fat eighth total of dark brown fabrics	Chocolate topping, melted chocolate, and cherry stem	Cut appliqué shapes from template patterns.
3" × 3" piece of red fabric	Cherry	Cut appliqué shape from template pattern.
7" × 7" piece of light blue fabric	Toppings jar	Cut appliqué shape from template pattern.
7" × 7" piece of transparent/ sheer tulle or chiffon fabric	Toppings jar	Cut appliqué shape from template pattern.
6" × 9" piece of gray fabric	Ice cream scoop and lever	Cut appliqué shapes from template pattern.
3" × 10" piece of blue fabric	Ice cream scoop handle	Cut appliqué shape from template pattern.
3" × 8" and 3" × 5" pieces of 2 purple fabrics	Sprinkles scoop	Cut appliqué shapes from template pattern.
½ yard fabric	Binding	Cut 5 strips, 2¾" × 42".
3 yards fabric	Backing	
Batting: 50" × 58"		

Other Notions, Tools, and Embellishments

- Ceramic bowl or plate
- Freezer paper
- Tear-away stabilizer for machine appliqué
- Open-toe appliqué foot
- Assorted embroidery thread
- Pinking shears
- 18" × 36" piece of wool or polyester batting for ice cream (optional)
- Gluestick or paper-backed fusible web
- Fabric spray adhesive for appliqués
- Beads, fusible rhinestones, permanent textile gem adhesive
- Buttons or sequins for "sprinkle toppings"
- Textile paints, paintbrush
- Hand sewing needle, strong thread for beads and embellishments

Purchase the larger amount if the fabric will not be 42" wide after removing the selvages.

Quilt Assembly

1. Fold the background into quarters, and press the crosswise and lengthwise folds.

2. Cut the ends of the 1″ narrow accent trim strips at a 45° angle, and sew end to end. Press the seams open. Sew the trim to the edges of the background fabric. See Adding Narrow Accent Trim to Mitered Borders, page 37, for details.

3. Sew the 4½″-wide striped border strips together, end to end. Press the seams open. Cut 2 strips 46″ long and 2 strips 54″ long.

4. Sew the borders to the background panel, mitering the corners. See Mitered Borders, page 34.

5. Fold each of the 3 background rectangles into quarters, aligning the corners. Position a ceramic bowl or plate at the corner, and rotary cut a curve to round the corners.

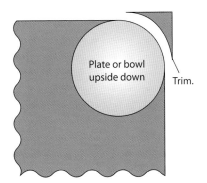

Plate or bowl upside down

Trim.

6. Position the largest rectangle on the background, aligning the horizontal center of the rectangle with the horizontal center of the background. Measure the exposed background on the top, bottom, and right side of the rectangle. Position the rectangle the same distance from the right side accent strip as from the top and bottom, approximately 2¼″.

7. Secure the rectangle to the background with straight pins, gluestick along the edges, or fusible web adhesive at the raw edges. Place a piece of tear-away stabilizer behind the rectangle. Machine appliqué with a decorative stitch. Remove the excess stabilizer from the back. If desired, snip the background fabric behind the appliquéd rectangle, and carefully cut away the background fabric to minimize bulk.

8. Fold the medium-sized rectangle in half horizontally and position it on the left side of the quilt top, centered with the horizontal center of the background and approximately 2¼″ from the left accent strip. It will overlap the first rectangle. Secure and appliqué to the background as in Step 7.

9. Add the smallest rectangle to the background, positioning it approximately 14″ from the left edge, 11″ from the top, and 9″ from the bottom edge. This rectangle overlaps the other 2. Secure and appliqué the rectangle to the background. Remove the stabilizer.

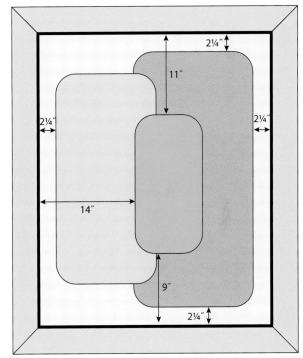

Rectangle placement diagram

ICE CREAM CONES AND SCOOP

1. Trace the template patterns from the pullout pages onto freezer paper, numbering and labeling the sections. Cut the patterns out along the drawn lines.

2. Using the half-diamond ruler or the template pattern on pullout page 2, cut 5 different cones from the brown fabrics.

3. Iron each freezer paper appliqué shape to the front of the chosen fabrics. Be sure that each ice cream scoop contrasts with the background rectangle behind it.

4. The ice cream "scoops" will be layered on top of one another. Cut out each scoop shape, adding a ¼" seam allowance along the upper edge of the lower scoops for layering. Refer to the pattern diagrams for guidance. Layer the double- and single-fabric ice cream scoops and secure the layers together with a gluestick.

Jan's tip

Optional embellishing: Use textile paint and a nearly dry brush to add subtle shading to give contour to the ice cream and create shadows on the same side of each cone.

5. Cut out the dark chocolate topping, and adhere it over the triple-scoop cone with a gluestick. Cut out and add the red cherry and brown stem to the double-scoop cone (cone 1).

6. Trim away any excess fabric on the back to prevent the darker colors from shadowing through the lighter colors.

7. Working outside or in a well-ventilated area, place the appliqués on a piece of cardboard and spray the back of each ice cream cone with fabric adhesive. Place the appliqué shape glue side down on polyester or wool batting, and apply pressure to adhere. Trim excess batting at the edge of each shape, angling the scissors to bevel the batting edge and prevent it from peeking out at the edges of the appliqué.

8. Position the padded appliqué shapes on the background. Refer to the quilt diagram on page 91 and to the photo on page 87 for placement guidance. Working on a flat surface, pin securely, allowing each shape to puff up slightly without distorting the background fabric. Machine appliqué each shape with tear-away stabilizer on the back, changing thread colors to enhance the various fabrics. Remove excess stabilizer.

9. Cut out the scoop from 2 shades of purple fabric. Adhere it to the background with temporary spray or a small piece of fusible web. Appliqué by machine using a stabilizer underneath. Embellish with machine satin stitching or couching if desired.

10. Cut out and appliqué the remaining shapes in the same manner. Consider personalizing your quilt with appliquéd lettering in the borders, such as "Super Scoops," "Happy Birthday," "Ice Cream Parlor," "One Scoop or Two?" "You Scream, I Scream, We All Scream for Ice Cream," "Everything's Better with Ice Cream," and so on.

11. Layer the quilt top with the batting and backing, and baste. Quilt by hand or machine with whimsical stitch patterns to fill the background and add contour to the cones and ice cream scoops. Bind, and add embellishments.

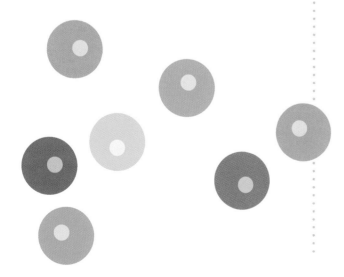

EMBELLISHMENTS AND SPRINKLE TOPPINGS

1. Embellish after quilting with any of the following options. Sew or use permanent textile adhesive to add:

- sequins, beads, rhinestones, small buttons, or ribbon "sprinkles" to enhance the ice cream

- natural stone "chip" beads to create chopped nut toppings

- charms, found objects, polymer clay shapes, specialty buttons, or teeny plastic spoons to the border

2. Cut the jar shape from tulle. Pin the tulle to the front of the quilt, angling the jar edges to allow a little fullness. Appliqué the left, bottom, and right edges to the background by hand, creating a pocket.

3. Sew a collection of beads, buttons, and sequins to a scrap of fabric or batting. Optional: Use textile adhesive to hold bits of plastic, tiny beads, or buttons on the surface of the opaque fabric, to create the appearance of the jar contents. Allow to dry. Slip the embellished fabric into the tulle jar pocket and sew the top closed. Optional: Trim the top of the jar with ribbon to enhance the design.

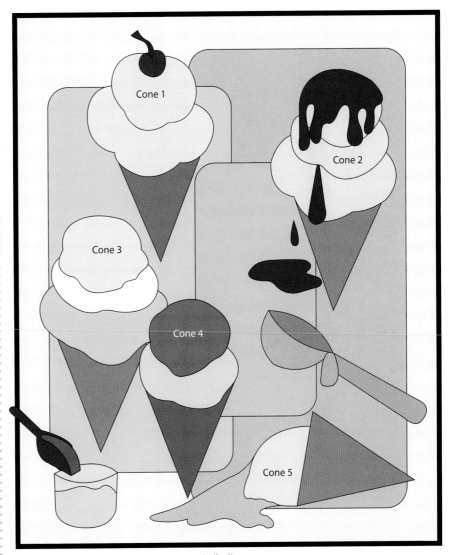

Quilt diagram

- Half-Diamond Thousand Pyramids
- fast2cut half-diamond ruler 6½"; or 6½" half-diamond template pattern and
Indian Summer half-diamond template pattern (pullout page P2)

Skill level: Skilled beginner

INDIAN SUMMER

55" × 62", 2008, by Jan Krentz; machine quilting by Janet Sturdevant Stuart, Fort Worth, TX

Think of those lazy late summer days, hazy with heat and the buzz of insects—perfect for a swim or a nap in the hammock! This quilt is a great scrap-buster—and a wonderful way to showcase your favorite fabric prints, batiks, and hand-dyed gradations. The classic Thousand Pyramids design typically features rows of triangles, all the same size. This version incorporates two triangle sizes, providing more visual interest and more economical use of fabric scraps.

Jan's tip

This design is easy to create as a smaller or larger quilt—simply add or remove rows. If you have a large number of fabrics, cut fewer pieces of each one. Fewer fabrics—cut more pieces of each fabric.

Fabric Requirements and Cutting

Refer to Prewashing Guidelines on page 9 to determine whether to wash your fabrics before cutting and sewing. Press all the fabrics with a light mist of spray starch to provide stability. See Cutting Half Diamonds, beginning on page 15, for details on cutting methods as needed, and Cutting Half Diamonds of Special Sizes, page 16.

YARDAGE	FOR	CUTTING
1½ to 1¾ yards total of light prints and batiks	Large and small triangles	Cut approximately 20 half diamonds, 6½". Cut approximately 120 Indian Summer half diamonds.
1½ to 1¾ yards total of medium prints and batiks	Large and small triangles	Cut approximately 20 half diamonds, 6½". Cut approximately 120 Indian Summer half diamonds.
1½ to 1¾ yards total of darker prints and batiks	Large and small triangles	Cut approximately 20 half diamonds, 6½". Cut approximately 120 Indian Summer half diamonds.
⅜ yard light fabric	Binding	Cut 4 strips, 2¾" × 42".
⅜ yard medium-dark fabric	Binding	Cut 4 strips, 2¾" × 42".
3¾ yards fabric	Backing	

Batting: 63" × 70"

Quilt Assembly

Be sure to read Construction Techniques, beginning on page 23, before beginning your project.

1. Arrange the large and small triangles in rows on the design wall. Refer to the quilt assembly diagram on page 94.

2. When satisfied with the arrangement, construct smaller "four-patch" triangle units and short diagonal rows made of 4 half triangles as needed. See Sewing Half-Diamond Units, page 28.

3. Construct rows of half diamonds and half-diamond units by sewing the pieces side by side. If necessary, mark the alignment dots on all 3 tips of the triangles to assist in accurately aligning the edges.

4. Press the seams open in each row, reducing bulk.

5. Join the rows together, aligning the half diamonds vertically over one another. Square up the quilt top, trimming excess triangles at the side edges of the quilt top.

6. Layer the quilt top with the batting and backing, and baste. Quilt as desired. Bind using the lighter strips along the lighter area of the quilt and the darker strips along the bottom.

Quilt assembly diagram

Laundering / Dye Treatment Products

Dharma Trading Company
(www.dharmatrading.com)
- Dharma Dye Fixative
- Synthrapol

ProChemical and Dye
(www.prochemical.com)
- Retayne

Grocery and drugstores, laundry department
- Shout Color Catchers (USA)
- Woolite Dye Magnet (USA)
- Zero Dye Magnet (Canada)

Rotary Cutting Rulers, Mats, and Cutters

C&T Publishing (www.ctpub.com)
- fast2cut Fussy Cutter 45° diamond rulers: 3" and 6½"
- fast2cut Half- and Quarter-Diamond Ruler Set

Omnigrid
- Invisi-Grip transparent film to prevent ruler slippage

Creative Grids USA

Olfa

Sewing Notions

Clover Quilting and Sewing Notions
(www.clover-usa.com)

June Tailor (www.junetailor.com)

Nancy's Notions
(www.nancysnotions.com)

Perkins Dry Goods
(www.perkinsdrygoods.com)
- Perfect Piecing Seam Guide

Prym-Dritz (www.dritz.com)

Fusible Adhesives and Stabilizers

The Warm Company
- Steam-A-Seam Lite
- Steam-A-Seam 2 Lite

Pellon
- Wonder-Under (USA)
- Bondaweb (UK)

Esterita Austin's Misty Fuse

Therm O Web, Inc.
- Heat'nBond Lite

about the author

Jan Krentz is a nationally recognized quilt instructor, author, and designer. She has been making quilts since the early 1970s and is a 1977 graduate of the University of Nebraska Textiles Department.

Jan is the author of *Quick Star Quilts and Beyond*, *Lone Star Quilts and Beyond*, *Hunter Star Quilts and Beyond*, and *Diamond Quilts and Beyond* and designer of the fast2cut Fussy Cutter diamond tools (all available from C&T Publishing). Winner of the 1998 Teacher of the Year award from *Professional Quilter* magazine, Jan offers motivating presentations and workshops that are packed with practical tips, techniques, and methods to ensure success. Her workshops and programs are in high demand; view her current schedule and workshops by visiting her website.

Jan lives with her husband, Don, in Poway, California.

Visit Jan's website, www.jankrentz.com; contact her by e-mail, jan@jankrentz.com; or write to Jan by postal mail:

Jan Krentz
P.O. Box 686
Poway, CA 92074-0686

Great Titles *from* C&T PUBLISHING

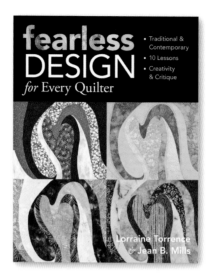

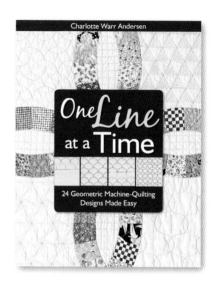

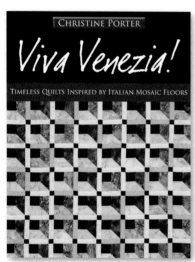

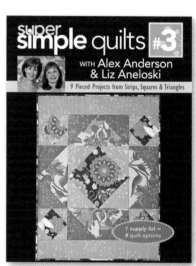

Available at your local retailer or **www.ctpub.com** *or* **800.284.1114**

For a list of other fine books from C&T Publishing, ask for a free catalog:

C&T PUBLISHING, INC.
P.O. Box 1456
Lafayette, CA 94549
(800) 284-1114

Email: ctinfo@ctpub.com
Website: www.ctpub.com

C&T Publishing's professional photography services are now available to the public. Visit us at www.ctmediaservices.com.

Tips and Techniques *can be found at www.ctpub.com > Consumer Resources > Quiltmaking Basics: Tips & Techniques for Quiltmaking & More*

For quilting supplies:

COTTON PATCH
1025 Brown Ave.
Lafayette, CA 94549
Store: (925) 284-1177
Mail order: (925) 283-7883

Email: CottonPa@aol.com
Website: www.quiltusa.com

Note: Fabrics used in the quilts shown may not be currently available, as fabric manufacturers keep most fabrics in print for only a short time.